THE BOOK OF CHANGING YEARS

A TIMELINE OF REAL AND PARALLEL EVENTS
AS WRITTEN BY AGENTS OF TIMEWATCH

with illustrations

PELGRANE PRESS
LONDON

CREDITS

Publishers: Simon Rogers and Cathriona Tobin

Authors:
    Heather Albano (Richard Plantagenet)
    Kennon Bauman (Ambrose Bierce, The Surgeon)
    Emily Care Boss (Liu Feiyan)
    Stephanie Bryant (Engineer Pritesh)
    Emily Dresner (Theodosia Burr)
    Marissa Kelly (Agent Snow)
    Emma Marlow (Lucas Lee)
    Epidiah Ravachol (Jacob Moyer)
    Rebecca Slitt (Edward Plantagenet)
    Ruth Tillman (Katia Filipovna, Publia Decia Subulo)
    and Kevin Kulp (Timeline)

Art Direction: Simon Rogers and Kevin Kulp

Cover Art: Sarah Wroot

Interior Art: Juha Makonnen

Design and Layout: Sarah Wroot

Endless Thanks:
    To every single Kickstarter backer who made this book possible. If it weren't for you, it wouldn't have been written, and we're grateful.

This book is dedicated to Simon Rogers, who embodied patience, kindness, and a steady hand forward – as well as the drive to launch TimeWatch out into the world. Thank you.

ISBN 978-1-908983-33-6

Pelgrane Press Ltd

Spectrum House, 9 Bromell's Rd,
London SW4 0BN, London, UK

© 2016 Kevin Kulp and Pelgrane Press Ltd. Ltd.
TimeWatch is trademark of Kevin Kulp and Pelgrane Press Ltd. All Rights Reserved.

PREFACE
&
INTRODUCTION.

I started tracking history when I became a TimeWatch agent. Not all of history, of course, only the parts I give a damn about. Here's the thing. A lot of prehistory is ridiculously boring, and there's a lot of room to hide in if you're trying to avoid someone. I mean, there's a billion years – a *billion* – when all of Earth is pretty much a big mat of bacterial slime. If you've ever been waiting for a SlideTrain and thought "oh man, this is taking forever!" because it was 15 minutes late, I advise you don't spend a lot of time in the Boring Billion.

But do you know what? Lots of history is also amazing, and there's untold amounts of amazing history that you've never heard of. There's heroism, drama, backstabbing, tragedy, pathos, unfairness, really ridiculous coincidences, and tiny pivotal moments that change the course of empires. For instance, the US Civil War was won by the North because some Union scout opened up a discarded cigar box and found Robert E. Lee's Special Order 191 wrapped around three cigars. Getting this secret plan for the invasion of Maryland to Union general George McClellan helped ensure Northern victory at the bloody Battle of Antietam.

And let me tell you, stealing those orders and leaving them in the cigar box for the Union to find at exactly the right time is exactly what being a TimeWatch agent is all about.

That's what I love, fixing the pivotal moments that other people screw up, and saving history when someone else tries to destroy it. That's why I started tracking some of those moments in history. I wrote them down here, along with the big occurrences you should probably know about. You won't find all the big events in history, just ones where I know time travelers got involved – and this doesn't even begin to cover all of the possible missions that are out there. There are hundreds of other amazing historical events taking place between each of these entries, and a little research on "timelines of world history" will reveal them to you in abundance. Every single one of those has an opportunity for adventure, or at least for a fast mission. The question is who'd want to change the event, and why? Answer that, and you're halfway there.

I'm writing this anonymously, because I'm spilling some secrets that aren't supposed to slip out. Just call me "the Historian" and know that I'm on the side of true history, whatever TimeWatch says it is, and I've done my best to make that

PREFACE & INTRODUCTION.

happen. And if I screwed up a few times? Well, no one's perfect, and erasing a paradoxical timeline means never having to say you're sorry to your briefing officer. Usually.

Over the years I've collected diaries and mission reports from other TimeWatch agents, and I'm including some of those here. There's a lot of missions at TimeWatch that no one ever talks about, and mysteries that no one has ever researched. Sometimes they're investigated or solved by agents from TimeWatch's future. Hey, that agent may even be you, looking at a future record of something you'll accomplish years from now.

I break the timeline down into Prehistory, Ancient History, Contemporary History, and Future History, but that's just for convenience. At TimeWatch, prehistory and ancient history are usually lumped into one category.

You'll find added mission summaries and stories here from a few different folks:

EDWARD PLANTAGENET, 17th Earl of Warwick, didn't die in the Tower of London in 1499 – and neither did his brother. Edward turned out to make a fine TimeWatch agent, and is a damn sight more honorable to his enemies than I ever was. Here he's tracking down chronal art smuggling and alchemy.

AMBROSE BIERCE the satirist offers his reflections upon being recruited.

AGENT SNOW is trapped between persecution, paranoia, and a vital mission. I included her formal logs into this timeline and journal to make a point: sometimes, changes in the timeline can work against you and you don't know whom to trust. Sometimes, time is cyclical.

THEODOSIA BURR, once called the best-educated woman in colonial America, was assumed lost at sea off the Carolinas. In truth, she now works for TimeWatch's Unfound Book Division.

LIU FEIYAN confronts the challenge of becoming emotionally invested in your work.

THE SURGEON is a freelancer who cleans up after TimeWatch when TimeWatch can't clean up after itself. When Atlantis starts to rise, he's the one who gets called.

PREFACE & INTRODUCTION.

PUBLIA DECIA SUBULO and her team haunt ancient Egypt, solving a plague of cats.

ENGINEER PRITESH and her team track the sentient fungus known as the Colony as it mutates into something even worse.

JACOB MOYER sees ghosts, ghosts that slip in and out of the currents of time. Tracking their source may be the most important thing he could possibly do.

LUCAS LEE presents an average week in the life of a TimeWatch agent, tackling multiple missions against unexpected odds.

KATIA FILIPOVNA's team tracks practical jokers through time, preventing historical sabotage through – of all things – pranks.

RICHARD PLANTAGENET... has had a tougher time being rescued than his brother. Let's leave it at that.

Their logs are arranged by their travel, not chronologically. It's easier to follow. CE means "Common Era" (what AD used to be); BCE means "Before Common Era."

One note. Your own future is always sketchy as hell, because it changes every time some two-bit chronal saboteur screws around with a plague or a filed-down firing pin on a sniper rifle. Our true future is pretty much what TimeWatch tells us it is, especially once the time machine is invented, and I've seen enough corruption within the ranks to know that I can't always trust what they tell me. You may find your own future to be dramatically different than what's listed here. Don't panic if it is; that probably means that whatever future I've experienced was wrong, and someone has altered it to its true path. I hope so, at least. Good luck with that.

The long unmeasured pulse of time moves everything.
There is nothing hidden that it cannot bring to light, nothing
once known that may not become unknown.
Nothing is impossible.

Sophocles, *Ajax*

CONTENTS.

TIMELINE.
Prehistory. – Ancient History. – Contemporary History. – Future History........ page 1.

EDWARD V.
2317 CE, September 23, Mars Colony Beta. – 2250 CE, Boston. – 2317 CE, September 24, Mars Colony Beta. – 2122 CE, August, Milan, Italy. – 1956 CE, May 4, Greenwich Village, New York. – 1956 CE, May 12, Greenwich Village, New York. – 1827 CE, Villa Montano, Florence, Italy. 1622 CE, November 25, Villa Montano, Florence, Italy. – 1622 CE, November 26, Florence. – 1622 CE, November 27, Naples. – 1150 CE, August 21, London. – 1150 CE, August 6, London. – 1150 CE, August 8, London. – 1144 CE, February 17, Toledo, Spain. – 1144 CE, February 18, Toledo, Spain. – 1956 CE, May 15, Greenwich Village, New York.... .... page 61.

AMBROSE BIERCE.
1913 December 26 .... page 79.

AGENT SNOW.
1903. – missing. – 1903. – missing. – 1903. – missing............................. page 85.

THEODOSIA BURR.
3700 CE, TimeWatch HQ. – 1521 CE, April 17, Worms, Holy Roman Empire. – 1492 CE, Barcelona, Spain. – 1476 CE, Republic of Florence. – 1417 CE, Convocation of Constance, Holy Roman Empire. – 1292 CE, January 11, St. Gertrude Monastery, Nyons. – 1292 CE, January 15, St. Gertrude Monastery, Nyons. – 1292 CE, January 17, St. Gertrude Monastery, Nyons. – 2348 CE, Neo New York. – 455 CE, March 5, Noviodunum, Western Roman Empire. – 1292 CE, February 9, St. Gertrude Monastery................ page 99.

JOURNAL OF THE SURGEON, AND OTHERS.
12584 BCE, August: Templeton Graves. – 1958 CE, November 16: Amelia Earhart. – 1958 CE, November 17: The Surgeon. – 1887 CE, March 18: The Surgeon. – 1968 CE, September 2: The Surgeon. – 2024 CE, August 3: The Surgeon. – TimeWatch HQ: Amelia Earhart. – 14 BCE, June 11: The Surgeon. – 1901 CE, April 21: The Surgeon. – 1961 CE, December 1: The Surgeon. – 1968 CE, September 29: The Surgeon. – 1958 CE, November 16 + 15 minutes: The Surgeon. – 1958 CE, November 16 + 16 minutes: Amelia Earhart .... page 119.

JOURNAL OF PUBLIA DECIA SUBULO.
1840 CE, London. – 648 CE, Lake Victoria, "Nalubaale," southern edge. – 2089 CE, Columbia University, New York City. – 637 CE, Yucatan Peninsula. – 2555 BCE, Third Cataract of the Nile, Kush. – 2586 BCE, Second Day of the Cattle Count, Memphis, Egypt.

CONTENTS.

– TimeWatch HQ. .... page 141.

JOURNAL OF ENGINEER PRITESH.
1986 CE, January 28. – 2012 CE, April 15. – 1986 CE, January 29. – 1986 CE, January 30. – 1862 CE, February 17. – 1986 CE, January 27. – 2009 CE, November 1. – 1862 CE, February 18. – 1984 CE, July 21. – 1984 CE, July 28. – 1985 CE, November 25. – 1985 CE, November 25, later that day. – 1961 CE, February 10. – 1961 CE, August 10. – 1863 CE, June 5. – 1962 CE, December 24. .... page 155.

JOURNAL OF JACOB MOYER.
1820 CE. – 247 BCE. – 1880 CE. – 20 CE. – 1972 CE. – 1158 CE. – 1936 CE. – 9430 BCE. – 2024 CE. .... page 169.

JOURNAL OF LIU FEIYAN.
4507 CE, Amundscott, Antarctica. – 2011 CE, Bohai Sea, China. – 2536 CE, Dronning Maud Land, Antarctica. – 3213 CE. – 2582 CE. – 4508 CE. .... page 179.

JOURNAL OF LUCAS LEE.
130 CE, June 15, Rome, morning. – 234,898 BCE. – 1919 CE, August 1, Paris. – 1914 CE, September 8. – 1914 CE, September 2, Châtillon-sur-Seine. – 1918 CE, August 1, Paris. – TimeWatch Citadel. – July 2223 CE, 2nd – 16th, São Paulo. – 130 CE, June 10, Rome. – TimeWatch Citadel. – 130 CE, June 15, Rome, lunch. – TimeWatch Citadel. – 2056 CE, July 4, New York. – 1928 CE, February 3, London. – 1911 CE, December 11, London. – 2055 CE, June 29, New York. – 2055 CE, June 29, Stanford. – TimeWatch Citadel. – 1978 CE, May 10, New York. – 1979 CE, May 10, New York. – 2138 CE, December 3, Hyderabad. – 2138 CE, November 21, Hyderabad. – 2138 CE, December 4, Hyderabad. – 1979 CE, May 10, New York, p.m. – 2138 CE, November 21, Hyderabad. – TimeWatch Citadel. – 1642 CE, August 29, Tortuga. .... page 189.

JOURNAL OF KATIA FILIPOVNA AND TEAM
1922, December 1: Katia Filipovna, New York City. – 1322 BCE: Katia Filipovna, Valley of the Tombs, Egypt. – 1922 CE, November 25: Katia Filipovna, Valley of the Tombs, Egypt. – 1922 CE, November 12: Katia Filipovna, Valley of the Tombs, Egypt. – 1922 CE, November 26: Katia Filipovna. – 2748 CE: Katia Filipovna, London, England. – 1800 CE, May 15: Fatima (Katia Filipovna's team), London, England. – 1800 CE, May 14: Fatima (Katia Filipovna's team), Residence of James Hadfield in London. – 1800 CE, May 15: Katia Filipovna. – 1301 CE: Mandy 9000 (Katia Filipovna's team), Pisa, Italy. – 1271 CE: Mandy 9000 (Katia Filipovna's team), 80.34 km west of Kashgar along the silk road. – 1271 CE: Katia Filipovna. – 1876 CE, March 10: Jun Kim (Katia Filipovna's team), Boston, Massachusetts. – 1876 CE, March 10, earlier in the day: Jun Kim (Katia Filipovna's team), Boston, Massachusetts. – 1876 CE, March 10: Jun Kim (Katia Filipovna's team). –

CONTENTS.

1865 CE, April 12: Katia Filipovna, Appomattox, VA. – 1839 CE, September: Katia Filipovna, West Point, NY. – 2748 CE: Katia Filipovna, Crabtree, TN. – 1839–1865: Katia Filipovna. – 2748 CE: Katia Filipovna, San Diego, CA. – 2746 CE: Katia Filipovna, San Diego, CA. .... page 205.

JOURNALS OF RICHARD PLANTAGENET AND THOMAS WU
3600 CE: Thomas Wu, TimeWatch headquarters. – 3600 CE: Thomas Wu, TimeWatch headquarters. – 3609 CE: Richard Plantagenet, TimeWatch headquarters. – 1483 CE: Richard Plantagenet. – 1486 CE: Richard Plantagenet. – 1487 CE: "Father Richard Symond" (formerly Richard Plantagenet). – 1488 CE: Edward Plantagenet. – 3612 CE: Thomas Wu, TimeWatch headquarters. .... page 221.

PRINTER'S NOTE
.... page 233.

INTERIOR ART
.... page 235.

TIMELINE.

PREHISTORY.

Prior to time	TimeWatch establishes its primary headquarters known as the Citadel inside the quantum anomaly that will eventually produce the Big Bang. It's a bold choice; the location is almost impossible to affect with chronal changes, but at some unknowable time we're going to accumulate too much paradox, destabilize the anomaly, and set off the birth of the universe ourselves. Inconvenient. We'll lose the entire organization's records, command structure, and infrastructure when it blows. I'm not sure when the paradox cascade gets triggered, or by whom, but I sure don't want to be in the Citadel when it happens.
	On the plus side, if you actually escape you'll have quite a story to tell your grandkids.
−13.8 billion years	Too much paradox accumulates in the Citadel, and the Big Bang occurs. The universe starts, everyone who runs this organization ends, and what's left of TimeWatch starts functioning without any sort of official backup.
−4.6 billion years	A whopping 9.2 billion years after the birth of the universe, the sun forms. That means our solar system has only been around for a third of the universe's life. Time machines or not, we haven't even begun to explore civilizations that rose and fell during this chunk of time. Here's hoping that none of them discover time travel, come forward in time, and discover us.
	The formation of the sun has been a surprisingly popular destination for astronomers and time tourists, despite no fewer than five separate expeditions being annihilated by a lack of understanding about where their craft should and shouldn't be during the big event. Questions abound, however, as at least two scientists believed killed during the primal supernova of the sun's creation have been spotted elsewhere in time – *changed*.
−4.54 billion years	The planets form, including a number of smaller planets with conflicting orbits.
	Until people began to understand chronal instability and the

TIMELINE.

deleterious results of skipping quickly through many years, time tourists were shown the formation of Earth by quickly making multiple time jumps for a "stop motion" effect. These were prohibited after expeditions simply faded away from chronal stability loss. We don't know how many expeditions vanished; the nature of chronal instability means that some expeditions (maybe hundreds?) ceased to have ever existed in the first place.

−3.8 billion years

Volcanic activity on Mars causes a build-up of greenhouse gases, leading to a heavy atmosphere and a water depth of some 120 m.

In the golden age of time travel (in other words, after it was discovered but before TimeWatch started reversing egregious and paradoxical use), time tourists paid fortunes for the opportunity to tour Mars by boat. Some entrepreneurs even tried to introduce terrestrial aquatic species to Mars for farming and breeding, with predictably disastrous results.

−3.7 billion years

Single-celled archaea are the first signs of life on Earth. Not interesting life, mind you, but an enemy heads here if they're determined to wipe out all life on Earth and stop it from ever forming. When a TimeWatch agent screws up and gets punished, being sent to watch over the beginning of life is one of those boring assignments that everyone dreads.

−3.26 billion years

Massive impact event when a 58 km. asteroid leaves a 480 km. diameter hole in what will eventually become South Africa. For reference, that's a crater two-and-a-half times the size of the impact that wipes out the dinosaurs. One theory suggests that this asteroid strike may be deliberately orchestrated by future TimeWatch agents to wipe out an Earth-dwelling alien threat.

−3 billion years

The moon is close enough to Earth that tides are 300 m. high, and the planet is hammered by constant hurricane-strength winds. If you visit, don't plan for good weather.

−2.3 billion years

Photosynthetic cyanobacteria churn out oxygen. That's pretty boring if you don't care about breathing, but if you do? Fascinating stuff.

Remember, bring your own oxygen on any time travel trips to early history. Oxygen may have triggered the evolution of more complex forms of life, and wiped out any forms of life that couldn't tolerate the stuff, but you still won't find our atmosphere easy to breathe for a billion years or so to come.

TIMELINE.

−1.8 billion years	"The Boring Billion." From −1.8 B years to −0.8 B years ago, Earth remains pretty damn changeless. Vast microbial mats of bacteria cover the planet, low oxygen prevails, and the massive violent environmental changes that characterizes Earth's earlier history calm down considerably. The Boring Billion is a time of unprecedented and unexplained stability.
	That makes me nothing if not suspicious. Maybe this stability was artificial. If so, why, and from whom? Was another race using Earth as a base at that point, maybe some sort of bacterial intelligence that wasn't preserved in the fossil record? There's a formal TimeWatch prohibition from going to look; you've got to hack your autochron to even reach that era. No one has told me why.
−850 million years	Want a snowball Earth where ice sheets actually reach the equator? The Cryogenian period starts around now, during which Earth freezes over three or more times during the next 200 million years. Life forms are still incredibly simple, developing slowly under the ice in locations of heat.
	TimeWatch has one unconfirmed report of cold-adapted aliens dwelling on Earth during this time, but if true they don't seem to have done any damage to the simple sponges and worms that were evolving. Let's hope none of them stuck around.
−555 million years	The first mollusk appears. Yaaaaay. TimeWatch sends agents back to stop time tourists and well-meaning scientists from kidnapping the first of the damn things as a souvenir.
−541 million years	Life forms start getting exciting (for certain definitions of exciting) as the Paleozoic period begins. Here's where we get fish (530 million years ago), trilobites (521 million years ago), and sharks (450 million years ago. Seriously, sharks, like beetles, are survivors). Right around sharks is when plants and arthropods head out of the ocean and onto land.
	I'm dumping almost 100 million years of life development into this one entry, but I think it's worth noting that there wasn't much for a time traveler to see if they weren't underwater. TimeWatch established a safe house in the continent of Gondwana around 500 million years ago, just in case any time travelers need somewhere relatively safe to gather before evolution starts to heat up. If you can, swing by. The chef's great.
−315 million years	The first reptiles evolve. Sophosaurs occasionally come back to this era to see their ancient, ancient ancestors; I guess humans aren't the only people prone to tourism.

TIMELINE.

−298 million years · All the continents are merged into the super-continent of Pangaea. This is about when beetles evolve, possibly giving way to ezeru in the unimaginable future.

−225 million years · Welcome to the Mesozoic and the Triassic! The first dinosaurs evolve about now. Five million years later flies and crocodilians come along, followed 5 million years after that by turtles and the first mammals.

It's important to note exactly how long dinosaurs existed: 165 million years. Read that again – 165 million years is a ridiculously long period of time, so long that the human brain has trouble even understanding it, and it's no wonder that sophosaur culture ended up so advanced. They had a lot of evolution to work with.

−201 million years · The Jurassic period begins, marked by an extinction event. The largest dinosaurs evolve in this period. So do the carnosaurs. If you want fast bipedal meat-eating dinos, here's where to start looking. Understandably, this period is popular with time travelers. Quite a few would-be dinosaur-riders get devoured instead, making this mostly a self-correcting problem.

−180 million years · Pangaea splits into two continents, Gondwana down south and Laurasia up north. Four million years later, stegosaurs develop. They end up being popular with super-scientists hoping to turn dinosaurs into cybernetic high-tech mobile platforms of war.

−145 million years · The Jurassic ends and the Cretaceous period begins. Over the next 80 million years you see the birth of the Atlantic Ocean, the first flowering plants, the first bees and ants, the first snakes, and (sadly) the first ticks.

−68 million years · The *Tyrannosaurus rex* evolves. Unlike the stegosaur, future super-scientists who come back to equip them with cybernetic weaponry find out that this is more difficult than it at first appears.

−66 million years · Killer meteor time at Chicxulub. *T. rexes* aren't around for long, evolutionarily speaking, as this extinction event ends the age of the non-avian dinosaurs. This is the event that changed history so profoundly.

Should the sophosaurs have evolved and the meteor missed Earth, as the philosoraptors claim? Did the meteor carry the first spores of the Colony to our world when it struck Mexico? Was TimeWatch involved with steering the meteor to ensure our own survival? This event has looped and entangled itself so many times

TOURISTS OBSERVE THE DINOSAUR EXTINCTION EVENT.

TIMELINE.

that the truth is no longer clear.

Either way, the mass extinction was not a pretty thing to watch – and I don't advise you stand near Mexico when the big day comes. It's not good for your health. A woeful number of tourists and scientists have found this out the hard way.

−49 million years — Whales return to the water.

That's probably not worth mentioning, except I was there when it finally happened, and it was pretty cool to see. If you show up and find me, I'll make you a drink.

−35 million years — Grasslands first appear. Isn't that a strange concept? But no vast rolling prairies of gently waving grass before now. Here's when we get dogs, eagles, hawks, and ground sloths.

−26 million years — The first real elephants evolve. Somewhere, an unborn Hannibal cheers.

−5.33 million years — The Zanclean Deluge occurs. This is possibly the best waterfall of all time; the Strait of Gibraltar opens for the last time, and water from the Atlantic rushes into the Mediterranean Basin. When I say rush, I'm not kidding, either; the entire sea fills in less than two years. If you want to go visit a truly awe-inspiring site, you could do a lot worse than this.

There was a Colony fungal infestation in the Basin just before this time. We believe the onrushing seawater wiped it out. You may find yourself on the TimeWatch cleanup crew to exterminate it with flamethrowers before the flood waters hit, and if you are, be damn thorough. Sentient fungus is an abomination.

−2.6 million years — The current ice age (known as the Pliocene-Quaternary Glaciation, which is not a good name for a band) begins. Ice advances and retreats on 40,000- and 100,000-year glacial periods. (Fun fact: the 21st century is in an interglacial period; the last glacial period ended about 8000 BCE.)

It's not long after the start of the last ice age that genus *Homo* appears. If you want to see *Homo erectus*, the really early "cavemen," here's where you go. Just keep your childish jokes to yourself.

−1.5 million years — Earliest possible evidence of early humankind controlling fire. A moment that's been parodied many times in bad caveman movies *actually happened*, when someone really used fire for the first time, and it happens around now.

TIMELINE.

Let's hope he or she didn't set themselves on fire.

−700,000 years — Earth's magnetic field reverses itself for the last time.

Alien plot? Natural occurrence? I'm no super-scientist; what I do know is that when it did, naturally occurring time rifts opened up all over the world to many different times, places, and parallel timelines. These mostly healed on their own after a few decades, but a few stuck around, and they're still occasionally causing problems for TimeWatch.

−640,000 years — The supervolcano in the Yellowstone Caldera erupts, collapsing in on itself and creating a giant crater 2,400 km² in area. Observe from a distance.

−250,000 years — Neanderthals evolve. There's another wave of mass kidnappings by future time travelers who want their own caveman as a conversation piece or lab rat. We here at TimeWatch work to discourage that, usually with heavy weaponry.

−200,000 years — *Homo sapiens* first appear in Africa. TimeWatch spends some time here preventing casinos from grabbing early *Homo sapiens* to use in high-stakes and highly publicized "cavemen fights," pitting modern against ancient human. Honestly, they're less exciting than you'd think – but I probably say that because we can pop into the future, find out who won, and then pop back into the past to lay our bets.

−170,000 years — Early humans start to wear clothing.

As expected, there was a brief and obnoxious period where the fashion industry regularly traveled back, dressed *Homo sapiens* in their designer duds, and took photographs and video for their marketing campaigns. That's just tacky, and we work to prevent it. There are some signs that a sophosaur clan is behind this, deliberately debasing human culture.

−75,000 years — The Toba event takes place at Lake Toba in Indonesia, when a massive volcanic eruption over 100 times greater than the 1815 Mount Tambora eruption (itself known as the "year without a summer") blankets Earth with ash and triggered a volcanic winter lasting 6–10 years. This sets off a 1,000 year cooling episode as well. If you're headed into the past for some beach-time rest and relaxation, I suggest you don't try it during the Toba event.

The important thing is that this led to the "genetic bottleneck theory," which basically posits that at some time in this period

TIMELINE.

humanity's ancestors were reduced to between 1,000 and 10,000 individuals total. There's genetic evidence for it, and the belief is that the Toba event pretty much killed every human on Earth except for a couple of thousand.

That's scary stuff because this is a massively vulnerable spot for humanity, and a huge opportunity for any enemy who can time travel and who wishes to erase humanity completely. Sophosaurs, I'm looking at you. Any enemy of humanity who wants to cleanse the planet would do worse than to bundle up in winter gear, head back to the Toba event, and finish off the job that nature started. It's our job to stop them.

−70,000 years — The earliest example of abstract art ever found, stones marked with a grid pattern, is left in Blombos Cave in South Africa. What you don't hear about are the stones marked with a call for help by stranded time travelers, hoping that their message is eventually found, publicized, and considered odd enough that a kind-hearted time traveler will come back to save them.

−40,000 years — *Homo neanderthalis* goes extinct. Sorry, Uurrk.

−26,000 years — The Last Glacial Maximum. In the same way that early 20th-century entrepreneurs took ice from New England lakes (especially Wenham Lake and Fresh Pond in Massachusetts) and shipped it around the world so that expatriate Brits in India could enjoy iced drinks on the veranda, time traveling ice and bottled water manufacturers head back to the ice ages to find pure water that they then sell at a profit. We keep an eye on them to make sure they aren't causing any unfortunate ripple effects by removing too many resources.

−25,000 years — North America is first colonized via the land bridge from Asia.

When the documentary crew surreptitiously filming this got spotted and killed by the colonists, TimeWatch needed to step in, save them, and deliver some advice about how not to be seen.

−15,000 years — The woolly rhinoceros goes extinct. I hope you get a chance to see one. My lord, they are magnificent.

−14,800 years — North Africa enters what's called the "Humid Period." Imagine the Sahara Desert wet and fertile, with all the reservoirs and aquifers full of water! There's a sophosaur clan living here during this period; it's not yet known if their psychic activity or even some sort of weapon is responsible for drying up the Sahara entirely.

8

TIMELINE.

−14,584 years   TimeWatch arranges for Atlantis' destruction and removal. It's a long story that no one will talk about.

−13,000 years   The climate warms and the glaciers begin to recede. This is also the period when Lake Agassiz is the largest lake on Earth, the size of the current Black Sea – then the walls break (we don't yet know why) and most of the water drains out into the Arctic Ocean through the Mackenzie River. It's no Zanclean Deluge, but it's still pretty damn impressive to see. If you're there, discourage thrill-seekers from trying to surf the flood.

−12,500 years   The oldest immortal I know of is born in Northern Africa. She hasn't aged since she hit early adulthood, and to the best of my knowledge she can't be killed. I have no idea why, but don't cross her or any of the other several dozen immortals out there. Most are very, very dangerous.

−11,000 years   Göbekli Tepe in southern Turkey is constructed, one of the oldest religious sites on Earth that survives to the 23rd century. This is also the period when Jericho emerges. That's interesting because Jericho is one of the oldest cities in the world that's been continuously inhabited. The walls of time are weak there, and echoes sometimes roll back and forth between the centuries. It's an unusual place.

Giant ground sloths and giant short-faced bears went extinct around now, partially due to 23rd-century poaching for a brief craze of using them as rich peoples' pets.

−10,000 years   The Quaternary extinction event occurs, when most of the ice age megafauna gives up the ghost and goes extinct. Your Irish elk, your cave bear, your big saber-toothed big cats . . . all gone. The mammoth manages to hang on in small islands until about 1700 BCE, lonely and isolated, but most of those go extinct now as well.

This is about the point when cultivation of barley and wheat began in ancient Mesopotamia. Don't get that excited. That early beer was awful.

−9,500 years   The cat becomes domesticated. Future unborn generations of Egyptians and Internet video watchers say a silent thank you.

−7,000 years   The wheel is invented and initial proto-writing begins to spread.

We've had a report that the wheel was invented after a late Neolithic village saw a time traveler use one, but we haven't been

TIMELINE.

	able to confirm that. The intelligent language Te'Pk tries and fails to get included in the proto-writing, but finds that the writing can't convey enough subtlety to maintain its intelligence.
–6,000 years	Civilization begins to develop in the Fertile Crescent region of Iraq between the Tigris and the Euphrates rivers. The horse is domesticated around now. So is the chicken, but that's perhaps less relevant to the future of mounted warfare – unless you're working with a really twisted bio-geneticist.
–5,900 years	Remember how I mentioned that the Sahara was wet and fertile? Here's when it rapidly dries up.
	We've long suspected that this has something to do with the sophosaur clan living in the region, either as a result of psychic weapons or some other root cause, but every agent we've sent to investigate hasn't returned.
–5,700 years	The Minoan culture begins on Crete. Actual Minoan art hasn't survived well, so you'll find a lot of chronal anthropologists (and art collectors) trying to learn about the civilization by inserting themselves as locals in disguise. They have mixed success, and we try to root out the smugglers.
–5,500 years	The first mummification in Egypt.
	Contrary to popular rumor, it wasn't inspired by ancient astronauts. Unfortunately, shape-shifting ezeru hoping to hide bodies of their paralyzed victims rely on mummification and sarcophagi to keep the individuals safe and disguised.

ANCIENT HISTORY

–5,200 years	This is a big one. Right about now, writing is invented in Sumer. That invention ushers in the beginning of history.
	Think about that for a second. Before we found time travel, everything we know about directly ... everything that ancient people could tell us about ... came from this point forward. My lord, did we miss a lot of amazing events before now that we have no way of knowing about unless we use a time machine!
	Cuneiform is the first writing system. Any writing you run into before this, especially rude graffiti and pleas for help, has probably been left by obnoxious or stranded time travelers. Head back and erase the graffiti (or rescue the stranded time traveler) when you have the opportunity.

TIMELINE.

It's at this stage that Te'Pk begins to spread from isolated pockets to whole communities, quickly knocked back by TimeWatch.

3200 BCE — The late Neolithic Cycladic culture of Greece rises up and faces infiltration from dozens of time traveling art dealers and mercenary art agents, all hoping to acquire the sculpture-like female idols carved out of white marble.

Paradox time: inspiration for the first idols might have been given by a time traveler who arrived early and didn't feel like waiting for the idols to be developed naturally.

3180 BCE — The Neolithic stone village of Skara Brae, one of the oldest settlements ever found by archaeologists, is founded in Scotland's Orkneys. It remains inhabited for almost 700 years.

As a known and ancient inhabited site, Skara Brae became a standard location for "first travel" by new time travelers until a narrow escape revealed that someone or something there is slaughtering every time traveler who arrives. The equipment stolen from these early time travelers has not yet been recovered.

3000 BCE — Construction of Stonehenge begins with a ditch, a bank, and 56 wooden poles.

Designed by disguised sophosaurs and powered with psychic emanations from religious rituals, these standing stones were eventually powerful enough to open a time gate. Whether the people who built them used the portal to travel to the past or the future, and who (if anyone) stopped them, is something that remains classified by TimeWatch.

2800 BCE (3300 BCE) — The Three Sovereigns and Five Emperors period begins in China. These mythological god-kings and sages are remembered as using their great wisdom and abilities to teach the people and improve the lives of their populace. They are said to have lived to a great age and brought great peace upon the land – which is fantastic until you suspect that they were probably time traveling rebels, former TimeWatch agents who defected to carve out an era of peace during a war-torn time. If that's true, agents are probably duty bound to stop them despite the consequences. This is one of those historical events that TimeWatch leadership hates, because who wants to risk agents defecting themselves when they're sent to stop something that arguably makes the world a better place?

2700 BCE — The Minoan capital city of Knossos reaches 80,000 inhabitants.

TIMELINE.

It falls 1,300 years later from the effects of a tsunami, but in the meantime Knossos becomes something of a melting pot and trade city for time travelers.

So little is known of Knossos that it's commonly believed that time travel there won't create paradoxes. If you need a safe place to meet someone with connections across the centuries, such as a smuggler or arms merchant, you could do worse than Knossos. Even the legendary labyrinth was an elaborate time trap to stop TimeWatch and other enemies from interfering. And hey, bioengineered minotaurs!

2700 BCE — Egypt's Old Kingdom first rises to power.

Ancient Egypt attracts power-mad time travelers like honey attracts ants, and no one is quite sure why; if you notice changes in the Egyptian depictions of their gods, here's where to look. Rumors that sophosaur and ezeru warfare inspired Sobek (the crocodile god) and Khepri (the beetle-headed god) remain pretty damn likely.

2650 BCE — The nation of Elam gains prominence in the location of southwest modern-day Iraq. Its matriarchal society becomes an inspiration during the Matriarchy Wars some 5,000 years later.

2560 BCE — King Khufu completes the Great Pyramid of Giza, assuming some damn time traveler doesn't replace it with a pyramid-shaped spaceship and TimeWatch has to fix things again.

Back when I was an agent, we had to do this twice. Seriously. And then they ended up trapping an ezeru queen deep beneath it, using the pyramid's energies to keep her trapped – don't ask me for specifics, I'm a field agent, not a chronal engineer.

I don't know if she's still there or not.

2500 BCE — Time traveling hunters drive the mammoth extinct, helped on by native hunters. Bastards, all of them. Luckily, mammoths still escape through naturally occurring time portals now and then, so we don't necessarily forget what they look like. Still, no one nowadays will ever know the wonder of seeing a massive herd grazing at dawn on a misty plain, or the wonder of hearing the bull trumpet challenge when he spots you, or the pants-wetting terror of the entire herd charging you while the ground shakes beneath your feet and you fumble for your autochron, praying you can fire it up in time not to be trampled.

I miss them.

TIMELINE.

2200 BCE — Stonehenge is finished. Finally.

An interdiction effect of unknown origin kicks in around this time; to know how it was used, agents will need to travel earlier and hike in overland.

2070 BCE — According to legend, Yu the Great establishes the Xia dynasty in China.

He was famed for an outstanding moral character and a focus on flood control – not sexy, perhaps, but the sort of thing people really appreciate. Written records in China didn't survive for nearly another thousand years, however, and he isn't depicted on contemporary artifacts. In truth? He was nearly erased from history due to chronal instability after a foolish time tourist made a very big mistake. We've never been able to fix the lack of records. If you're reading this and you think you can, good luck to you.

1800 BCE — Alphabetic writing (okay, Proto-Sinaitic script, but close enough) first shows up on the Sinai Peninsula. If someone completely changes the very nature of writing, start here and work forwards to track them down.

c. 1780 BCE — The legendary Tower of Babel is a Babylonian city completely infected by Te'Pk, with a massive tower stretching to the heavens covered with inscribed Te'Pk that continues infecting humans for thousands of years to come.

TimeWatch stepped in and utterly destroyed the time loop, removing the Te'Pk infestation at its source. Legends of a common tongue and a huge tower lingered regardless.

1600 BCE — The Minoan civilization on Crete is destroyed by the aftereffects of the volcanic eruption of Santorini (then named Thera). The resulting tsunami throws the Minoans into disarray, making them easy military targets for the militaristic Greece Mycenaeans. If you run into chronal thieves smuggling ever-rare Minoan art, they won't likely be active later than this.

1200 BCE — The Bronze Age begins to collapse in the Eastern Mediterranean and Southwestern Asia. Trade routes disappear, literacy drops, and the "palace economy" becomes cultures of isolated villages. Numerous cities are violently destroyed and left unoccupied. Troy, for instance, is destroyed twice and left abandoned until Roman times. The *Iliad* and the *Odyssey* are written 400 years later but are set in this period.

TIMELINE.

Due to a series of secret-but-fairly-stable time rifts that appeared for several decades in the 22nd century, the Bronze Age collapse briefly became a convenient place to dump bodies slain in purges by despotic governments.

800 BCE The rise of the Greek *polis* (city-state) eventually leads to a flourishing of culture and art. Self-interested art dealers come back in time to provide protection services to specific artists.

The alternate timeline leading to Alexandrians diverges during this period, although we've never figured out exactly where or how.

776 BCE The first recorded Olympic Games occur in 776 BCE in Olympia.

Hopefully, they occurred without an influx of future time tourists trying to observe or show off by competing themselves! Held in honor of Zeus, only free-born Greek males (or time travelers who could successfully impersonate them) were allowed to take part. An Olympic truce period lasted up to three months before and during the games, allowing spectators and athletes to travel safely. Chronal saboteurs who attempt to disrupt this have historically been treated harshly by TimeWatch, in part because the games are secretly televised back in the Citadel and we hate interference.

753 BCE The traditional founding of Rome.

If your changed history features Reme instead of Rome, someone screwed with the original founding myth of the half-divine twins Romulus and Remus. Check here.

For the record, they weren't truly divine. My advice? Any time someone claims to be descended from a god or a demigod, check for chronal radiation. You'd be amazed by how many times some self-involved time traveler with delusions of grandeur attempts to pass themselves off as a Greek or Roman god. Embarrassing, really.

700 BCE The beginning of five centuries of the Chinese "Hundred Schools of Thought," when numerous schools teach competing and conflicting philosophies and differing ideas are freely discussed. I may be prejudiced, but some of TimeWatch's most successful and interesting agents come from this period. Who doesn't like wandering scholars and philosophers passing between kingdoms to advise state rulers?

This period ends 221 BCE with the imperial Qin dynasty and something known as the "purge of dissent," which is exactly as

TIMELINE.

much fun as you'd think. Legend holds that the first Qin emperor buried 460 Confucian scholars alive in 210 BCE after many books were burned. Recruitment believes that at least some of these scholars would make good TimeWatch agents.

612 BCE Nineveh, the largest city in the world (over 100,000 inhabitants), is destroyed by an alliance of its former subjects: Babylonians, Chaldeans, Cimmerians, Medes, Persians, and Scythians. The Assyrian Empire soon follows suit.

The last days before the allied armies reach the city are a frenzy of art smuggling by time travelers. It's believed that several of these anachronistic travelers are slain by the locals, and the location and disposition of their time machines is unknown.

586 BCE Solomon's Temple, the First Temple in Jerusalem, is destroyed by Babylonians. This has become a magnet for time traveling zealots (and, to be fair, the better-behaved faithful) of multiple religions. Millennia-spanning religious conspiracies have their birth in this event.

563 BCE Buddha, born Siddhartha Gautama, is born as a prince in ancient India's Magadha kingdom. He soon becomes the target of numerous assassinations from fanatical time traveling cults hoping to change history. It's to TimeWatch's credit that none have yet succeeded, at least for long.

551 BCE Confucius, who obviously founded Confucianism, is born in 551 BCE. Bet you didn't know he was a contemporary of the Buddha!

More than one over-ambitious tourist has tried to get the two of them to meet, mostly through blatant kidnapping. We disallow such things, especially when we hope to someday recruit Confucius as a TimeWatch adviser.

546 BCE Remember the phrase "rich as Croesus"? Well, Croesus is king of Lydia in 546 BCE, and Cyrus the Great (founder of the Persian Empire four years earlier) defeats him and orders him to be burned to death on a pyre.

Legend holds that Croesus was rescued by Apollo himself and taken away to the Hyperboreans; there's a pretty good chance that "Apollo" looked a lot like someone interfering on a time machine, but no one has yet proven it.

509 BCE The Roman Republic is founded, and the last king of Rome, Lucius Tarquinius Superbus (Tarquin the Proud), is exiled. You

TIMELINE.

can barely cross the city without tripping on a chronal historian trying to finish their dissertation. Sadly, that also means there are saboteurs and shape-shifters hidden during this time who hope to reshape the Republic. Sometimes the two groups are indistinguishable.

508 BCE Athens institutes democracy, and Soviet and Chinese Communist time travelers from three different centuries do their damnedest to stop it. We step in to surreptitiously lend a hand at rounding up both the Communists and the well-meaning civilians from other countries who attempt to stop them.

500 BCE The intelligent and parasitic language Te'Pk tries to sneak into Pānini's text that standardizes Sanskrit into what's now called Classical Sanskrit. The result almost colonizes India's wisest scholars into an inhuman hivemind of shared and dominated flesh.

499 BCE The Greco-Persian Wars kick off thanks to King Aristagoras of Miletus, who may or may not have a shape-shifted adviser. The Battle of Marathon, and the Battles of Thermopylae and Salamis, follow in the next 20 years. Xerxes the Great isn't assassinated due to palace intrigue until 465 BCE.

I remember the Battle of Marathon (490 BCE) because my own squad of TimeWatch agents got called in to stop a heartbroken 23rd-century scientist whose daughter suffered a heart attack while running a marathon. The scientist tried to stop the Greek messenger Pheidippides from running to Athens with news of the battle, a classic case of overkill if I've ever heard of one. We were able to restore history (and the road race), calm the scientist, and at least give her the opportunity to say goodbye to her daughter before that 23rd-century road race. It's nice that not every mission involves shooting someone.

432 BCE The Athenian Parthenon is completed after 15 years of construction. Every once in a while, particularly vain time travelers try to get themselves carved into the temple's sculptures instead of the original models. Still, that's not as bad as the time travelers who show up in multiple paintings and sculptures from a number of different eras, "art-bombing" history until agents can catch up with them.

I may be sensitive to this, though. A time traveling graffiti artist (and a personal nemesis) left insulting comments about me in over three dozen works of art and antiquity before I managed to track the guy down. Worse, TimeWatch recruited him instead of punishing him! That was when I retired to become a librarian and write these entries, and do you think anyone is ever going to read them? Hah!

I need a way to get this out to the agents who will find it actually useful. Maybe 19th-century London. But anyways, the Parthenon. Right. Very pretty.

400 BCE — The Zapotec civilization thrives in the Oaxacan valley of Mexico near Monte Albán. It is around this time that a rogue sophosaur tribe secretly arrives seeking refuge. The sophosaurs ingratiate themselves to the Zapotec leaders and live amongst them for a time before striking out into deeper jungle. If you can infiltrate without being spotted by sophosaur spies, the site in Monte Albán is gorgeous, with psychic amplification architecture you'll never forget. Literally. The sophosaur-enhanced architecture burrows into your brain and makes you unaccountably loyal to the city, possibly giving the philosoraptors minor control over you as well. Be cautious and plan accordingly.

399 BCE — Socrates dies. Fifteen years later in 384 BCE, Aristotle is born. If you head back to talk philosophy with either of them, don't forget your MEM-tags

331 BCE — The Etemenanki, a centuries-old massive 91-meter-tall ziggurat dedicated to Marduk in Babylon, is demolished on orders from Alexander the Great (with perhaps some assistance from a few undercover TimeWatch agents). This coincidentally destroys a hidden source of Te'Pk writing.

323 BCE — Alexander the Great dies in Babylon at age 32.

Don't let any histories tell you otherwise; he was poisoned. The question is, by whom? And did the poison kill him or render him apparently dead – and if the latter, who wanted to kidnap him to use as a general for their own futuristic army? He'd be a brilliant leader, particularly if trained in modern or futuristic tactics and logistics. But did we grab and recruit him, or did one of our many enemies?

I'd find out myself if I still had access to my autochron. But mark my words, there's foul play here, and I'm not entirely sure it didn't originate with a time traveler.

300 BCE — Possibly under sophosaur direction, the largest pyramid by volume in the world (the Great Pyramid of Cholula in Mexico) begins construction. The question is, why are the sophosaurs involved at

TIMELINE.

all? It's possible that this is all misdirection to pull TimeWatch into a trap, so proceed carefully.

202 BCE — The Battle of Zama turns out to be crucial for Rome's survival, as (war elephants and numerical superiority be damned) Scipio Africanus defeats Hannibal. This marked the end of the Second Punic War and turns out to be a favorite spot for meddlesome time saboteurs who want to change Roman history. Beware of Carthaginians bearing beam weapons and woolly mammoths instead of elephants.

146 BCE — Rome wins the Third Punic War and completely razes Carthage. This is also the year that Greece is conquered. It's no surprise that the Alexandrians (alternate reality Greeks) have it out for Scipio, is it?

44 BCE — The Roman Republic ends, and the Roman Empire begins, as Julius Caesar is murdered by Marcus Brutus and his collaborators.

Lots has been written on this, and this is another event that saboteurs (and even well-meaning time tourists) tend to interfere with. Caesar was stabbed 23 times, and some 60 men were involved with the plot; you can bet that not all were from that time period. I've even had to shut down a huckster's "Come stab Caesar!" time tour that was particularly egregious, and I can't imagine that was the only one.

40 BCE — The Romans conquer Egypt, at least in our true history. There are lots of variants here, including some where Queen Cleopatra lives and thrives, and some where Rome doesn't make it past the attempt. If you happen to run across Queen Cleopatra, say hi to her intelligent talking cat for me. It tends to ramble, but it serves her as a remarkable adviser.

4 BCE — Jesus of Nazareth is born, and don't even get me started on the number of time tourists, saboteurs, or zealots who want to interfere with *that*. We have an interdiction device set up to slow them down, but it's a popular destination that's remarkably difficult for all the TimeWatch teams standing by to protect. Like in 1940s Berlin, teams have to take a number to deal with each successive threat, and teams are quickly cycled in and out so that their paradox from repeatedly encountering themselves doesn't become excessive.

HANNIBAL TURNS THE TIDE AT ZAMA.

TIMELINE.

9 CE — The imperial Roman army gets their collective asses handed to them in the Battle of the Teutoburg Forest. This battle is studied by military tacticians, and if you show up there you'll probably find the nearby trees full of surreptitiously placed spy cams filming the action. This is the battle that keeps Germania independent of Roman rule.

27 CE — The crucifixion of Jesus Christ occurs around this period. If there's a time period that gets swarmed by time tourists (assassinating Hitler aside), it's this one. TimeWatch has placed an interdiction device up around this period as well to try and keep out the casual time travelers, but that won't stop the more innovative or dedicated faithful. We keep a safe house and field office there so that there's enough personnel to identify time travelers and intervene when necessary.

41 CE — The Roman Senate expresses their displeasure with the unstable Emperor Caligula by having him assassinated. He's succeeded by his uncle Claudius. You'll find some sybaritic pleasure-seekers infiltrating Rome in this period, but it doesn't usually end well for them.

43 CE — Rome first enters Britain. Come for the weather, stay for the silver mines!

54 CE — Back in Rome, Claudius dies and his grandnephew Nero – you know, of the supposed "Nero fiddled while Rome burned" – takes the reins of power. A 23rd-century reality HV (holovision) show loads Rome down with hidden cameras and mics and tries to create a real-life period drama. After *Livia* did so well it seemed like a sure win, but other time travelers interfere to bring about their own plot line resolutions, leading to its cancellation.

68 CE — Yeah, that didn't last long. Nero kills himself, and the infamous Year of Four Emperors begins in Rome. This is a textbook case of political machination, and worth a visit if you can find the time.

70 CE — The armies of Titus destroy Jerusalem. Jerusalem is an interesting place. The walls of time are shaky there, a lot like Jericho, and people often feel closer to the divine while they're there. Are they? I'm not sure, but I do know it's the location of one of the few location-based mental illnesses. Research "Jerusalem syndrome," and you'll wonder about it as much as I do.

TIMELINE.

79 CE	Mount Vesuvius erupts, and Pompeii pays the price.

Some TimeWatch agents were killed in that eruption, and there are rumors that they were betrayed by a rebel triggering a short-term interdiction device that prevented escape. If that mystery has been solved the truth may be classified, as I've never heard about a resolution.

106 CE	The Roman Empire reaches its largest size under Emperor Trajan, invading and conquering modern-day Armenia, Romania, and Iraq.

We saw a strange outbreak of something appearing to be vampirism around this period – doubtlessly bioengineered in the future and brought back as an infectious disease into Romania – but let me tell you, preventing the Roman army in Romania from turning into a vampiric horde was not my favorite mission of all time.

Eleven years later Trajan dies of natural causes, and definitely not vampirism. He's succeeded by his adopted son Hadrian, as in "Hadrian's Wall." The size of the empire shrinks as Rome pulls out of Armenia and Iraq.

220 CE	The Han dynasty falls in China, and the Three Kingdoms period begins. This lasts until 280 CE and is remarkably bloody. Think I'm kidding? Not so; other than World War II, it's considered the deadliest period in history, with a census showing 80% of households – some 8 million – being destroyed during this time. A lot of interesting technological advances, though. Cold comfort.
285 CE	Diocletian becomes the Roman emperor and splits up the empire into the Eastern and Western Empires. A deliberate persecution of Christians begins in this year as well.

It isn't until 313 CE that the Edict of Milan declares that the Roman Empire would accept (or, perhaps, put up with) all forms of religious worship – and don't think that numerous fanatics haven't tried to go back in time and change *that*.

330 CE	Constantinople is named after the Emperor Constantine and becomes the capital of the Eastern Roman Empire. Later it becomes Istanbul, not Constantinople, Istanbul, not Constantinople… darn it. Now I have that song stuck in my head.
335 CE	In India, Samudragupta becomes the emperor of the Gupta Empire. He's considered to be an astonishing military genius whose rule begins the Golden Age of India. He kills 9 rulers and

TIMELINE.

conquers another 12 during his military campaigns. Any rumors that he is invincible in battle due to advanced technology are almost certainly scurrilous. If you're lucky, you can find a way to train under him for military tactics.

406 CE — The Romans are forced out of Britain. It is a bad period for the Romans; a year later, in 407, Germanic tribes such as the Visigoths cross into Roman-controlled Gaul, and King Alaric of the Visigoths sacks Rome a few years later in 410. That's the first time Rome is sacked in almost 800 years. Not the last, though.

I've seen one case where a socially regressive senior citizen used a time machine to send neighborhood Goth teenagers back in time to this period, so that they could "meet real Goths!" Don't do this. It ends badly for everyone.

455 CE — Vandals (the tribe, not the miscreants named after the tribe) sack Rome after conquering most of North Africa.

Time travelers join the looting, hoping to get their hands on statuary and valuable antiquities that wouldn't otherwise be missed. Some Vandals get their hands on those looters' time machines, leading to a chronal rampage up and down the time stream. Solving this one took longer than you'd think.

476 CE — The fall of Rome. This is considered the end of European ancient history, when the last Western Roman Emperor is forced to surrender to a Germanic chieftain named Odoacer. No fool, Odoacer exchanges the imperial regalia for the title of dux of Italy, granted by Emperor Zeno of the Eastern Roman Empire. All in all, nice maneuvering. That imperial regalia is a prime target for time thieves.

c. 500 CE — Welcome to the Middle Ages! Time travelers obsessed by – okay, that's a little strong, let's say "enthusiastic about" – the legend of King Arthur head back to England for the Battle of Mons Badonicus. Legend has it that King Arthur is involved, but that's not much more than hearsay. A surprising number of casualties in the battle turn out to be historical re-enactors.

524 CE — If you want to influence early Christianity, or if you want to stop someone else from doing so, go meet Boethius while he is jailed by the king of the Ostrogoths. His *Consolation of Philosophy*, written in prison, becomes one of the most influential books of the Middle Ages.

TIMELINE.

525 CE	The Anno Domini era (used by the Gregorian and Julian calendars) was triggered by the Scythian monk Dionysius Exiguus' calculation for the dates of Easter. When someone wants to mess with the calendar, they occasionally head to influence Exiguus directly.
529 CE	The Eastern Roman emperor Justinian I publishes his *Corpus Juris Civilis* (*Body of Civil Law*).
	This is what saboteurs occasionally corrupt or change when they wish to change the foundation for some modern civil law. Justinian I was an interesting guy who sought to recapture the lost Western Roman Empire. He managed it well, using superb generals to conquer the Vandals and Ostrogoths and re-establish control over Rome's lost lands. If you see him, tell him I say hi; we've become fast friends.
532 CE	The Nika Riots in Constantinople are used by ezeru to feed extensively. Half the city is burned, tens of thousands are killed, and the ezeru behind it are never caught.
c. 570 CE	Muhammad is born. His revelations from God are recorded in the Qur'an, and give rise to the religion of Islam. When he dies in 632, all of Arabia is Muslim. Understandably, this is another period under interdiction to keep out the faithful who are on a chronal pilgrimage.
581–618 CE	Over in China, the Sui dynasty unites China for the first time in four centuries. It doesn't last long, but it ushers in new prosperity and the spread of Buddhism across the country.
	The Grand Canal is built during this period, and it's known that the chief architect actually turned down assistance from a time traveling engineer. That engineer is still on the run, probably making herself into a nuisance elsewhen.
590 CE	Gregory the Great becomes the pope. If anyone ever changes Gregorian chants or the Catholic liturgy, head back here to see if foul play is afoot.
650 CE	The same Native North American lives his life 17 times, being repeatedly reborn into the same body in something akin to auto-reincarnation. TimeWatch can't determine why, but realizes that he's definitely not the only one. We recruit him.

TIMELINE.

711 CE — Arabs and Berbers come up from North Africa to invade the Iberian Peninsula. Muslims rule the area for more than the next 700 years. There's at least one parallel timeline where they continue to advance and capture all of Western Europe.

732 CE — The Battle of Tours.

You'll care about it because it was here that Charles Martel stopped the Muslim advance into Europe. If this had gone differently, the Franks may have never had the Carolingian Empire. (Go research the names of the rulers of the Carolingian Empire, by the way; they're great.)

754 CE — The pope is promised central Italy by Pepin the Short, and the Papacy begins to achieve true military and state power. Anti-religious time travelers hoping to undermine the Catholic Church occasionally try to step in here to undercut the Papacy.

768 CE — Charlemagne's reign begins. He was the first Holy Roman Emperor, and his remarkable rule set the stage for modern France and Germany. He only reigns for 13 years, but he still gets referred to as the "Father of Europe." Not a bad legacy.

I've been told that a time traveler picked him up the morning of his death and took him forward to see his legacy; not sure if that's true, but I hope it is. Every once in a while it's worth breaking the rules to be kind to someone remarkable. I feel the same way about Ada Lovelace in 1852.

800 CE — Gunpowder is invented. If you run into it before this, it's probably anachronistic. Note that guns aren't invented for some time afterwards.

850 CE — The golden age of the Buddhist Srivijaya Empire in Southeast Asia. Based in Sumatra, it's strongly tied to the spread of Buddhism.

When it fell in the 13th century, it lay forgotten until the beginning of the 20th century – but it's regained popularity as a destination for time travelers curious about South Asian politics, trade and religion. We even had to dig out an anachronistic 25th-century ruler who had come back to "live the good life" and glorify himself. Jerk.

866 CE — The Viking "Great Army" pays a call on England and conquers as it comes.

If you need to recruit a Viking to TimeWatch, there are plenty of

TIMELINE.

smart and capable candidates who otherwise perish in the invasion. Careful, though; at least once a time rip opened up in front of this army and they ended up somewhere else. That's been fixed, but it could easily reoccur.

868 CE	The earliest known book with a date is published in China. TimeWatch has scrubbed out time tourist graffiti in the margins several times.
885 CE	Vikings attack Paris. No one ever talks about that normally, do they?
900 CE	The Mayan Empire disintegrates, partially fueled by internal division over the inclusion of rogue sophosaur clans as advisers.
955 CE	Otto the Great defeats the Magyars at the Battle of Lechfeld, preventing the Hungarians from entering Central Europe. Battles like this, which significantly stop large invading forces, are common linchpins targeted by historical revisionists or saboteurs. Change the victor, and whole ethnographic groups and national boundaries tend to shift.
985 CE	Erik the Red begins colonizing Greenland after he is exiled from Iceland. He discovers Greenland to be a verdant paradise ruled by intelligent dinosaurs; after TimeWatch steps in to root out the sophosaur clan, and after paradox sorts itself out, he actually discovers Greenland to be the frozen hellscape we know today. Doubtlessly, a small part of his altered memories is terribly disappointed.
989 CE	The Catholic Church tries to control society through nonviolent means instead of through strength of arms. The "Peace and Truce of God" uses spiritual pressure to clamp down on war, and is the first time this occurred in medieval Europe. Futuristic observers embedded in the church keep a sharp eye out for anachronistic meddlers in the process.
1000 CE	The turn of the millennium, and some villagers huddle under a winter sky, sure that the end of the world is coming. In several now-corrected timelines, they are correct.
1001 CE	Leif Eriksson winters in maritime Canada, becoming the first known European to stop in the Americas. Native American assassins from the future try to assassinate him as a political statement.

TIMELINE.

1021 CE — *The Tale of Genji,* by Murasaki Shikibu, is completed by now. It's considered by some to be the world's first novel, if you don't count all the knockoffs published by egocentric time travelers in the few years preceding this.

1049 CE — Pope Leo IX becomes pope. He's worth mentioning because he and the patriarch of Constantinople excommunicate each other, leading to the Great Schism in the Catholic and Orthodox Churches. I find this hilarious, even if it wasn't as much fun to be there in person.

1050 CE — The astrolabe gets invented, and navigation gets significantly easier. Chronal rifts out at sea start being discovered, leading to all sorts of confusion. If an explorer heads to 1050 CE, they're going to find more than one ship and plane straight out of the Bermuda Triangle.

1077 CE — Construction starts on the Tower of London. If you ever need to influence its design – and time travelers have dozens of times for all sorts of reasons – this is when to head.

1095 CE — Pope Urban starts the Crusades to recapture the Holy Lands. This is the first of nine over the next few centuries. They turned out to be an efficient way to kill off many of Christianity's finest warriors, and I'm still not convinced they aren't a complex ploy to do exactly that.

1117 CE — Oxford University is founded. It's ridiculously old, isn't it? There's a time machine hidden somewhere deep beneath Oxford, but the chronomorphic disguise hiding it makes it ridiculously difficult to identify.

1118 CE — The Knights Templar is founded to guard Jerusalem and to protect pilgrims to the holy lands, thus giving rise to innumerable conspiracy theories over the later centuries. The best warriors are slowly separated from the order and dropped off in a null-time "waiting room," waiting for the day when they'll be called to duty.

1122 CE — Emperor Henry V and Pope Calixtus II draw up the Concordat of Worms. I mention this not for the bitter rivalry this failed to solve, but for the fact that "Concordat of Worms" is a fantastic name. That's all. Carry on.

1193 CE — The university at Nalanda in India is burned and sacked by Turkic Muslims. Buddhism begins to decline in India as a result.

TIMELINE.

It isn't uncommon to see interested parties trying to save the university, thus delaying or preventing the change in religious focus. What people don't realize is that a battle of wills between the Colony and a Te'Pk infestation made the fire a necessity. Sometimes you really, really need to burn things to the ground. And don't even get me started on the Library of Alexandria.

1204 CE — The Byzantine Empire starts its decline as Constantinople is sacked during the Fourth Crusade. Two years prior, the Catholic crusade also sacked the Catholic city of Zara. Never underestimate a soldier's greed for the spoils of war.

We saw ezeru activity here as well, snatching locals as food during the military action.

1206 CE — Genghis Khan is elected khagan of the Mongols. Say goodbye to political borders and a whole lot of heads, as the Mongols proceed to conquer most of Europe and Asia. So many people are descended from Genghis Khan – approximately 1 in 200 men in the early 21st century – that his life becomes a massive pivot point for time travelers to try and affect.

1215 CE — The Magna Carta is sealed by John of England. Up until now it's almost unheard of for a medieval ruler to accept any sort of limit on their authority, so this sets a remarkable precedent. We see the occasional demagogue trying to reverse this action.

Also in 1215, the Fourth Lateran Council ruled that Muslims and Jews needed to wear identifying marks so that they could be told apart from Christians. This set an awful precedent, one that I'd gladly reverse if I was allowed to. No wonder agents join the rebellion.

1227 CE — Genghis Khan dies, and his empire is divided between his children. His extremely charismatic third son Ögedei is declared to be the great khan, but only if he reduces his alcohol intake to one cup of wine a day. Ögedei, a clever ruler indeed, agrees – and has a massive cup made so that he can stay true to his word.

1242 CE — The Mongol expansion into Western Europe is checked at the gates of Vienna, where messengers reach Batu Khan with news of Ögedei Khan's death. The vast army decamps overnight, returning to Karakorum to determine the next khan.

Vienna must have thought they'd been spared by God. In truth, I was one of those damn messengers for months of hard travel, forced into the position after a Korean chronal saboteur killed the originals. A lot of good it did, too! Another saboteur saved Ögedei

TIMELINE.

from dying of alcoholism, and an entirely different team of agents was needed to save Western Europe.

In dreams, I can still smell horse and leather.

1279 CE   The Song dynasty in China ends after the Battle of Yamen, and Kublai Khan becomes emperor of all of China.

Shangdu (Xanadu), the capitol of the khan's Yuan dynasty in China, was just as amazing as Coleridge dreamed it would be.

1297 CE   William Wallace participates in the Battle of Stirling Bridge, and rises as the leader of Scottish resistance against England.

He wasn't wearing a kilt or using blue face paint, but he was one hell of a warrior. I had a mission in the area at the time when someone tried to sabotage Scottish independence, and I enjoyed the man.

1298 CE   Marco Polo publishes details of his journeys into China. His stories capture the public imagination and bring Asia and Europe closer in trade.

More interestingly, there was a 27th-century competition for a time between young time travelers who each tried to alter Polo's account, adding in more and more outrageous lies – with the winner forced to alter history to make those lies become truth.

1299 CE   The Ottoman Empire is founded, and it lasts over 600 years. It ends the Byzantine Empire (in 1453), it stretches across continents, and it lasts until the end of World War I. Not too shabby.

CONTEMPORARY HISTORY

1307 CE   Remember the Knights Templar? They're gathered together by Philip the Fair of France with the pope's support, and (barring the ones drawn away into a null-time place of waiting) they're murdered. The order falls within a decade.

1310 CE   Dante publishes his *Divine Comedy*, including his *Inferno*.

Time travelers try to get themselves inserted into his work, and there's some belief that Dante was actually brought to a 22nd-century Italian Hell-themed amusement park before he wrote his *Inferno*. I don't buy it, but someone may have made the attempt.

1325 CE   The Aztecs found Tenochtitlan. The city lasts until Cortés invades some 200 years later. It's amazing to realize that Oxford

TIMELINE.

University was founded some 200 years *before* Tenochtitlan.

1337 CE — England and France begin the Hundred Years' War. It actually lasts 116 years, but that's partially due to a chronal bobble and an accidental paradox. Hostilities rise and fall over generations. Interfering time travelers set themselves up as multigenerational advisers to the major players.

1347 CE — The Black Death makes its first appearance in Europe and kills somewhere between 20 and 40% of the population in the first year alone. By the time it's done, some 50% of the population is dead. This is a time of terror when a number of TimeWatch's enemies try to expand their power; the Colony grows on corpses, ezeru scavenge bodies, and sophosaurs work to shape culture in the power vacuum of dead and terrified aristocrats.

I'm telling you, everyone tries to manipulate history by messing with the plague. For one thing, it's incredibly effective, but it's like swatting a bumblefrog with power armor. Plague is undiscerning in who it takes, and unless you manage your inoculations carefully it has a bad habit of growing out of control.

1368 CE — The Mongol Empire breaks up, ending the Pax Mongolica. Two years later and Tamerlane begins his successful 35 year battle to restore the Mongol empire. Nostalgia and national pride can be bloody.

1378 CE — Three popes, no waiting? The Western Schism elects multiple popes simultaneously. Several time travelers vie to take part in the struggle for control, leading to a brief but memorable alternate history nicknamed "Popemaker" that boasts no fewer than 17 simultaneous popes. It's quickly sorted out before TimeWatch gets involved.

1380 CE — Chaucer begins to write *The Canterbury Tales*, instrumental in establishing modern English speech. The sentient language Te'Pk somehow gets included in the tales, starting parasitic colonization across time – mostly in English professors.

1405 CE — Zheng He begins the first of his seven naval expeditions sponsored by the Ming Empire.

In at least one of these expeditions, a paradox occurs when Zheng He is tipped off to the Pacific Gyre and accidentally discovers the west coast of North America. TimeWatch steps in to prevent inadvertent Chinese colonization of America, but never finds the

TIMELINE.

saboteur who revealed the new continent's existence.

1415 CE — The Battle of Agincourt, where Henry V and his small army use English longbows to beat the larger French army.

Charles VI didn't command his army personally because he was remarkably mad, suffering from conditions such as glass delusion (where he thought he was literally made of glass and might shatter. Did you know that at one point, Charles VI didn't bathe or change his clothes for five months? Learn from my mistake and try not to meet him in poorly ventilated chambers).

1431 CE — Joan of Arc is tried and executed, if you consider "recruited to TimeWatch" as "executed."

1434 CE — The Medici family starts making waves in Florence. The Medicis become rulers, bankers, and popes (really bad ones, too) across Europe for the next three hundred years. We've recruited a few, and so have our enemies; if you approach them, make sure you can scheme as well as they can. You may also want to make sure they're human; we've found reptoids, sophosaurs, and ezeru pretending to be Medicis at one point or another.

1439 CE — Gutenberg invents the printing press, and Te'Pk immediately moves in to take advantage of the discovery.

1485 CE — Richard III dies in battle at Bosworth Field, except for the times that someone has given him anachronistic force armor. In true history, Henry Tudor is declared king of England.

1492 CE — It's considered a rite of passage for Native American time travelers to try and stop Christopher Columbus from reaching the New World. It doesn't solve the problem, but the quest is both symbolic and highly satisfying. It's our job to stop them – kindly and safely, if we can.

1501 CE — Michelangelo returns to Florence and begins work on *David*. Disguised time travelers compete to become the model, becoming flat-out annoying for the sculptor. He moves onto the Sistine Chapel ceiling in 1508–1512.

1503 CE — Nostradamus is born in Saint-Rémy-de-Provence, Provence, France. He either has access to a time machine or an anachronistic adviser; no one has ever decided which. It's even possible that he is a disguised time traveler himself. His prophecies continue to

TIMELINE.

vary in accuracy as interested parties try to manipulate events to prevent them or make them come true.

1506 CE — Leonardo da Vinci finishes the *Mona Lisa*. This is another case where the time tourists (and would-be thieves) become annoying until TimeWatch steps in. It works, too; the actual model is rumored to be a TimeWatch agent, which is definitely against normal protocol.

1517 CE — The Sweating Sickness becomes an epidemic in Tudor England, brought in by an ill and unwary time traveler. It kills several thousand people this year alone. A year later in 1518, some sort of nonhuman mind control creates the Dancing Plague in Strasbourg.

1519 CE — Hernán Cortés heads off on the Spanish conquest of Mexico. This ends badly for Mexico and the Aztec. As with most of the conquistadores, this piece of history twists and turns as rebels attempt to reverse the damage that Europeans did to their native populations. We see this around the world as well, in China and Korea and India and in innumerable smaller countries, as well-meaning patriots try to save their original culture. It really is no surprise that well-meaning agents join rebel groups to assist them.

1520 CE — Smallpox arrives in the Americas, carried by an infected African slave on a Spanish ship sailing from Cuba. The disease (and other European diseases) sweeps across North America and kills some 96% of the native population, somewhere between 40 and 90 million people. In most scenarios where the Europeans never colonize North America, it's because of mass antibiotics brought in by angry time travelers.

1521 CE — Global circumnavigator Ferdinand Magellan is ostensibly killed by warriors in the Philippines. In related news, he makes a superb agent.

Manuel I, king of Portugal, dies in this same year. He's notable for creating the first global empire. I think most people forget that Portugal was an earthshaking world power at this time, and that they'd earned it.

1531 CE — Atahualpa and Huáscar fight the Inca Civil War only a year before Francisco Pizarro leads Spanish troops to conquer the Incan Empire. Rebels inoculate Incans against European diseases while releasing some highly targeted diseases of their own on the Spanish; under some ethical duress, TimeWatch is forced to step in.

TIMELINE.

In an incredibly clever bit of plotting, one of the rebel groups goes back in time to convince Pizarro to start his conquest, and deliberately gets spotted by TimeWatch. Their theory is that if it's shown that a time traveler actually started the conquistador off, maybe we'd jump to conclusions and prevent the whole conquest. As it turned out, however, Pizarro turns out to be a murderous conquistador just fine on his own, so our hands were tied.

1541 CE — We're well into the Age of Exploration, and the Amazon River is explored by Francisco de Orellana. Sophosaur clans stalk him through the jungle and eliminate his party entirely, requiring TimeWatch agents to go back in time, join his group, and provide undercover security during his expedition.

1548 CE — The Ming dynasty orders all Chinese ports closed to foreign trade. The goal is to prevent piracy, but the result is to impoverish coastal communities.

We believe that ezeru used this as an opportunity for a feeding frenzy as desperate inhabitants were forcibly moved to new locations.

1556 CE — The Shaanxi earthquake in China becomes the Ming dynasty's deadliest known earthquake, killing approximately 830,000 people. An ezeru queen is disrupted by the tremors, and thousands of ezeru warriors burst from the ground in affected areas. The carnage is terrible.

1558 CE — Queen Elizabeth I is crowned at age 25. She ushers in the height of the English Renaissance, and future historians agree to take turns imitating a single one of her courtiers so that people can have equal access to Her Majesty.

1560 CE — Countess Elizabeth Báthory is born in Hungary. A prolific murderer, she kills hundreds of young girls and possibly bathes in their blood to maintain her youth. Bricked into her prison cell, she escapes with a time traveler the night before her death; TimeWatch covers up the escape and continues to hunt both the countess and her mysterious collaborator.

1566 CE — The great sultan Suleiman the Magnificent dies at the age of 71, leaving 30 million citizens in the Ottoman Empire. His grand vizier keeps the death secret for a time to avoid poor morale during battle.

It's believed that Suleiman knew the truth about time travel, and

TIMELINE.

	regularly entertained witty visitors and magnificent storytellers who arrived and departed in secret.
1582 CE	Pope Gregory XIII ends the Julian calendar and begins the Gregorian calendar. The days between Thursday, October 4, 1582, and Friday, October 15, 1582, completely disappear. These dates are now used by time travelers who desperately need to hide.
1592–1598 CE	With the help of the Ming dynasty, Korea successfully defends against 158,000 Japanese troops and two Japanese invasions. Both Korean and Japanese time travelers try to turn these wars to their own nations' advantage.
1600 CE	The British East India Company is granted a charter by Elizabeth I, and England begins a mercantile and military expansion into Asia. I've seen a few time travelers try to seize control of this company, to use it towards their own military or political ends. It's seldom that they're wily enough to succeed, however, unless they step in with a tether and take the role of logistical adviser.
1601–1603 CE	A Russian famine kills about 2 million people, one third of Russia's population, throwing the country into chaos. Scavenging ezeru appear, stealing bodies and briefly impersonating important people who had not yet died. The famine is linked to the eruption of the volcano Huaynaputina in Peru.
1605 CE	"Remember, remember the 5th of November ... " The Gunpowder Plot fails, and time traveling subterfuge now surrounds the event. When it comes to Guy Fawkes, don't necessarily trust anything you hear – even if it's from his own mouth.
1606 CE	Another moment in the Age of Exploration that draws some resentment, this is the year that the sailors on a Dutch East India Company ship named the *Duyfken* becomes the first known Europeans to make landfall on Australia.
1607 CE	Jamestown, Virginia, becomes North America's first permanent English colony. Substantial effort is put into changing that by 22nd-century Native American scientific leaders who acquire time travel.
1610 CE	François Ravaillac assassinates King Henry IV of France. A Catholic zealot, he experienced a (time traveler inspired?) vision in 1609 that the king should convert the Huguenots to Catholicism.

TIMELINE.

When he couldn't get close enough to the king to tell him of his vision, he lay in wait and stabbed the man instead.

1616 CE

William Shakespeare dies.

I'm still resentful that TimeWatch agent Mace Hunter tried to change *Macbeth*'s title to *Macebeth*, and got nothing more for it than a slap on the wrist. Hmmph.

1627 CE

Aurochs go extinct. Sorry, guys.

1629 CE

Cardinal Richelieu works against Ferdinand III in the Thirty Years' War, and fans throughout history of *The Three Musketeers* pick their new time travel destination.

1633 CE

Galileo Galilei arrives in Rome before his Inquisition trial for espousing heliocentrism. He's eventually forced to recant and lives out the next nine years under house arrest in Florence.

1642 CE

The 5th Dalai Lama wins a civil war and joins with the Khoshut Khanate to create a civil administration in Tibet. Tibetan Buddhism spreads; a sophosaur clan gathers to see if human culture has any redeeming features after all.

1665 CE

The Great Plague of London, in which 100,000 people (a quarter of London's population) die. This is followed in 1666 by the Great Fire of London.

Someone really had it in for London.

Also in 1665, Portuguese forces behead King Nvita a Nkanga (António I of Kongo) at the Battle of Mbwila. When West Africa becomes a popular spaceship port in the 24th century, Restorationists act to travel back and reverse this indignity.

1687 CE

Isaac Newton publishes his book *Philosophiæ Naturalis Principia Mathematica*. The scientific world takes a step forward out of superstition.

1692 CE

The Salem Witch Trials occur in Massachusetts. No one gets burned at the stake – most are hanged, one is pressed to death – but don't be surprised if someone with a personal axe to grind comes back and interferes with the trial, either to use science to prove that witchcraft actually exists, or to save the victims. This is a small historical event that some people still feel strongly about.

1702 CE

Forty-seven ronin attack Kira Yoshinaka in Japan. Before they can

TIMELINE.

	commit *seppuku*, a time traveler spirits them all away. No one is yet sure why, or for what purpose.
1709 CE	The coldest winter in some five centuries is called the Great Frost of 1709, and it triggers a famine that causes 600,000 French deaths. The Swedish invasion of Russia is badly compromised due to the cold.
	We have reason to believe that it was engineered by weather manipulation, but no one yet knows by whom or why. It's even possible that we triggered it on purpose, although I can't imagine why.
1712 CE	The very first shipment of Javanese coffee reaches Amsterdam. Caffeine-deprived chronal anthropologists who are embedded there let out a sigh of relief.
1718 CE	Notorious pirate Blackbeard (Edward Teach) is killed off the coast of North Carolina.
	He was – but he went time traveling while he was younger, so he's still out there sailing the seas of time.
1720 CE	The South Sea Bubble becomes a major financial crisis, and time-hopping speculators try to jump in on the action or get their ancestors out before it is too late.
1739 CE	The War of Jenkins' Ear is fought by Great Britain and Spain over trading opportunities in the Caribbean. This isn't particularly a chronal pivot point, but it does have a great name.
1755 CE	The Lisbon earthquake shatters Portuguese coastal fortresses and somewhat puts an end to the age of Portugal's world dominance.
1765 CE	British Parliament forces the Stamp Act on its American colonies. While this has been revoked by rogue time travelers hoping to prevent or delay the American Revolution, it's been reinstated by – of all things – ezeru who wish to ensure nuclear development 180 years later in the USA. Sometimes, the enemies of your enemies ...
1769 CE	Napoleon Bonaparte is born on Corsica. He has a constant TimeWatch guard on him, but that's not enough to stop multiple assassination attempts.
1775–1783 CE	The American Revolutionary War begins. There are innumerable pivot points during the war, both with battles and leaders.

TIMELINE.

	TimeWatch goes on a recruitment binge, rescuing brave and smart but otherwise doomed soldiers before they can be killed. The Marquis de Lafayette is recruited regardless.
1783 CE	The Mist Hardships in Iceland, when a volcanic eruption creates famine that kills a quarter of the population. At least one rebel group has gone here for recruits, saving doomed Icelandic citizens and training them for war against TimeWatch.
1798 CE	The Quasi-War is fought at sea between France and the United States' shipping.
	Knowledge of the war is suppressed by sophosaur mindwhips acting with some sort of amplifier, but we still can't remember (or understand) how they were involved in the first place.
1799 CE	Undermined by systematic mismanagement by time travelers' local agents, the Dutch East India Company is bankrupt and dissolved.
1801 CE	Alexander Hamilton decides the US presidency for Thomas Jefferson, instead of Aaron Burr, when there's a tie in the Electoral College.
1803 CE	The Louisiana Purchase more than doubles the size of the United States, triggering the philosophy of Manifest Destiny that drives American explorers and settlers to conquer new territories from their native inhabitants. As expected, anyone looking to cripple the United States' growth looks at this purchase as an excellent opportunity for sabotage.
	Also in 1803, Britain and France declare war, one more step towards the Napoleonic Wars. The Russo-Persian War starts the next year.
1804 CE	The world's population hits one billion people. This date wavers depending on how many plagues get past TimeWatch's notice at any one time.
1805 CE	The Battle of Trafalgar wipes out French and Spanish fleets, setting the stage for British dominance of the oceans. As the British Empire expands across the world, this advantage grows in importance. Patriots love to come back and change this outcome, but it's so obvious that it quickly gets corrected unless the saboteur is particularly subtle.

TIMELINE.

1811 CE	Time traveler Gideon Montoya founds the isolated town of Longtree South Dakota, neutral ground for time travelers that's used as a refuge for those on the run.
1812 CE	In the War of 1812 between the United States and Britain, Native Americans lose the most power; 23rd-century diplomatic talks later discuss whether or not retroactive remunerations (by going back in time and setting things to rights) are the just and legal step to take.
1815 CE	Napoleon experiences his Waterloo, and the Napoleonic Wars draw to a close.
1816 CE	The Year Without A Summer (following the eruption of Mount Tambora) results in the creation of Mary Shelley's *Frankenstein; or, The Modern Prometheus*.
1820 CE	Antarctica is discovered; initial explorers are found infested with Europan tongue parasites. TimeWatch steps in to burn them out.
1828 CE	Tasmania's Black War almost wipes out its aboriginal population. It takes a rapidly fading Tasmanian TimeWatch agent from the 22nd century to come back and identify the anachronistic warmonger using advanced persuasion techniques to encourage escalating violence.
1831 CE	The HMS *Beagle* is sunk by fervent anti-evolutionists from the future. We step in to lend a hand and restore things to rights.
1835 CE	The Republic of Texas varies in length depending on who tries to arm and advise the separatists. For instance, Texans win the Battle of the Alamo when they're supplied with futuristic weapons and force fields to use against Santa Anna.
1838 CE	I wish I could say the Trail of Tears was false history that we could reverse. I so wish I could.
1841 CE	Richard Owen coins the word "dinosaur." Sophosaurs across the globe furrow their eye ridges.
1842 CE	The British retreat from Kabul, Afghanistan, through the Khyber Pass. Under Major General Sir William Elphinstone, 16,500 British soldiers and camp followers set out; fewer than five make it through. More than one soldier has tried to repair the worst

TIMELINE.

British military disaster known to that point.

1848 CE — The battle for women's suffrage is begun at the Seneca Falls Convention. Occasionally, ignorant jackasses will try to reverse this. We let all-female TimeWatch teams deal with them when this occurs. It seems *apropos*.

1850 CE — Ending in 1864, the Taiping Rebellion in China results in the death of some 20 million people. This is another great place to lose a body if you need a good disposal location.

1856 CE — *Homo neanderthalensis* is first identified. Ironically, one of the discoverers is TimeWatch agent Uurrk, a Neanderthal himself, disguised and working under deep cover.

1861 CE — The US Civil War begins, also known as the War Between the States and the War of Northern Aggression – although not all at the same time. In true history it ends in 1865 with a Northern victory. TimeWatch fights a constant series of battles to keep this consistent, as many saboteurs hope to change or reverse the war's results.

1867 CE — Dynamite is invented by Alfred Nobel. One sophosaur clan's propaganda quickly encourages people to use the explosive indiscriminately. The results, soon reversed, are horrific.

1873 CE — Japan abolishes the samurai class. Many samurais are rapidly recruited into TimeWatch and various rebel organizations.

1876 CE — Great famines in India and China (some 40 million people eventually die of starvation and disease) are a painful counterpoint to the Gilded Age in American culture. Social agitators from the future begin sneaking thousands of armed Indians and Chinese into United States cities via temporary teleportation portals; TimeWatch is forced to unravel the conflict from the beginning, but never catches the agitators behind it.

Also in 1876, General George Custer is killed at the Battle of Little Bighorn. Supporters occasionally try to lend him a hand with some air support or anachronistic weapons. Don't let them.

1879 CE — Edison invents the lightbulb, and don't even get me started with Edison and Tesla.

We *had* to address Tesla's competence; he was smart enough to develop his own super-science, and destroying his death ray and earthquake machine was best for everyone. I still feel a little guilty about the pigeon infatuation, though, a side effect of too much MEM-tagging. We should have recruited him instead.

1881 CE	The Gunfight at the O.K. Corral echoes into history as an iconic Old West event.
	I was somewhat impressed when they turned it into a documentary in the hopes of keeping away tourists.
1883 CE	Krakatoa explodes, one of the loudest sounds known in modern times; the sound wave is so loud that it passed all the way around the world four times.
	The volcano might have been set off by workers from the future, but no one wants to get close enough to find out.
1885 CE	King Leopold II of Belgium seizes the Congo Free State through brutality. More than one freedom fighter has tried to kill him first.
1888 CE	The Jack the Ripper murders begin in Whitechapel.
	The killer blunders into a working time machine and escapes to 1970s San Francisco; the inventor, surreptitiously aided by TimeWatch, is forced to track him down. News of this mission slipped out due to faulty MEM-tagging, and eventually ended up as a movie.
1890 CE	The American Old West draws to a close at the Wounded Knee Massacre. Indigenous American tribes continue to look for unassailable pivot points from which they can rewind history. Tourists – and yes, I do have some scorn set aside for them, don't I? – continue to come back for souvenirs and tragic memories. Sorry, I'm not usually this bitter. The first thing you learn at the Citadel is that history is seldom if ever fair. That doesn't make it easier.
1896 CE	The Olympic Games return to Athens. Time travelers, returning the favor, smuggle in a few athletes from the original games in 776 BCE.
1897 CE	Bram Stoker pens *Dracula*, but few people realize that it's nonfiction. TimeWatch continues to fight isolated outbreaks of vampirism across the centuries.
	I heard a rumor that an agent was infected and fled on his autochron to find Dracula himself; if true, it explains the massive scramble they had just before I was recruited, and the sudden openings I observed when multiple agents died suddenly and

TIMELINE.

permanently from "top secret causes."

1900 CE — The 1900s are largely defined by an increase of speed: speed of travel, speed of inventiveness, speed of communication, speed of convenience, and speed of information. You see this theme throughout the century, and most of our threats are trying to either reverse this trend (such as the occasional sophosaur clan) or accelerate it even more (such as ezeru attempting to trigger Armageddon). When it comes to chronal threats, the 20th century is a busy time indeed.

1901 CE — Queen Victoria dies, ending her age.

An attempt to turn Victoria into an undying bioengineered self-replicating cyborg just before her death was thwarted with minutes to spare. A different attempt to salvage her brain for a floating steam-powered braincase was slightly more successful and required additional intervention. Sometimes I have little patience for alternate realities invading our own.

1903 CE — The Wright brothers get their airplane off the ground, a first step in ushering in the era of air travel. Other contenders, such as Clément Ader in his bat-winged device, take a back seat in the official history books – unless someone clocks in to interfere.

1908 CE — The Tunguska impact shows exactly what happens when a time machine malfunctions.

We still don't know who the victim is or how the tragedy occurred, but it flattened thousands of square kilometers of Siberian forests. There's still a pulsing hole in space and time up there that no one can sense.

1910 CE — Halley's Comet returns, somehow opening multiple time rifts across the globe. By the time they close, hundreds of people have gotten lost in history.

1912 CE — The RMS *Titanic* sinks. This is particularly worrying because the exact event was foretold in a book called *Futility, or the Wreck of the Titan*, written in 1898 by US author Morgan Robertson.

1913 CE — Adolph Hitler, Emperor Franz Josef, Leon Trotsky, Tito, and Josef Stalin all live in Vienna at the same time in 1913–1914.

Together, they were responsible for some 80 million deaths. Sigmund Freud lived there too, although it's fair to say he was less political.

AN AGENT IS RECRUITED,
SAN FRANCISCO EARTHQUAKE 1906.

TIMELINE.

1914 CE In a nearly botched assassination that had to be carefully manipulated by time travelers, Gavrilo Princip starts the Great War (World War I) by assassinating Archduke Franz Ferdinand in Sarajevo.

This is also the year that the last passenger pigeon dies. A suggestion: go back in time and stand under the open sky, with the warm wind in your face, when the birds turned the heavens black for hours and hours as they flew overhead. To do so is to understand the passing of time, and the ending of things, and the unthinking cruelty of man.

1916 CE Daylight Saving Time is instituted in order to give chronal refugees an extra hour to hide in, 60 minutes when no one can find them. The hour is cleaned out every six months, dumping refugees back into the world – but it's good to have a chronal bolt-hole when you really need one.

1918 CE World War I ends, and the borders of nations are redrawn. We see a lot of interference with time travelers trying to wrangle a better deal for their own personal nation. Petty, I think.

1920 CE American Prohibition begins, prohibiting alcohol in the US. This turns out to be just as popular as you'd probably expect.

1921 CE As the Roaring Twenties take hold, Adolph Hitler becomes führer of the Nazi party. We've had to implement round-the-clock protection of someone truly loathsome, and we try to do so with a minimum of interdiction devices. That's how you know you've really screwed up at TimeWatch: round-the-clock Hitler duty. You watch him from midnight to 7:59:59 a.m., clock out, get some rest, clock back in at 8:00:00 a.m., watch him until 3:59:59 p.m., clock out ... *ad nauseum* for months. Whatever you did, you'll never repeat the infraction. I guarantee it.

1924 CE Lenin's death sets off a power struggle for Stalin and Trotsky. The loser is the Russian people.

1928 CE Penicillin is invented by Alexander Fleming.

An attempt to avoid 22nd-century overpopulation involved killing Fleming as a youth. Trust me, that doesn't solve the problem.

1929 CE The Wall Street crash sends the USA spiraling into the Great Depression. The age of classic American mobsters continues, with

TIMELINE.

bootlegging leading to particularly organized crime. We see a lot of historical revisionism in this time period, as people desperately try to get their ancestors out of the market before it crashes. Everything is interconnected, however, and paradox usually blossoms after someone tries to make a change in their own fortunes without considering anyone else's.

1933 CE — Global economies and governments are still reeling from the end of the Great War, and we see the results as true history and interfering saboteurs work against one another. Over the next few years Hitler rises, Stalin begins his Great Purge, Mussolini invades Abyssinia, Japan invades China, Mao Zedong begins the Long March, and the world pretty much goes to hell. My advice? Focus at one problem at a time, fix it, and move on. It's too easy to get swept away in paradox if you try to see the big picture here.

1934 CE — A German archaeologist in Iraq discovers the Jemdet Nasr, a sentient lapis lazuli ring acting as the prison for an alien entity known as Pi'drak. Those who touch it begin seeking power, often through physical force. It circulates within the Middle East and Central Africa for generations before TimeWatch is able to track it down.

1936 CE — Edward VIII becomes king of England; sadly, the woman he falls in love with (Wallis Warfield Simpson) turns out to be a reptoid and he soon abdicates.

1939 CE — Nazi Germany invades Poland, starting World War II in Europe. The Soviets invade Poland 16 days later. Time travelers secretly reinforce Polish troops with anachronistic weaponry, at least until we catch them – and then it's nearly all-out war between us and several allied rebel groups, even as the world war rages on around us.

1941 CE — How many times have people tried to change Pearl Harbor? Too many times. The war rages, and many changes come quickly. Luckily for the Allies, someone convinces Hitler that it'd be a great idea to invade the Soviet Union.

1942 CE — Inspired by disguised ezeru, the Manhattan Project begins.

1944 CE — The first electronic computer comes online. Colossus is used for cryptanalysis.

Its power is quite limited except for one late night when pranksters replaced its output with that of a modern TimeWatch tether;

43

TIMELINE.

	the late-night technician never managed to convince anyone of the holographic wonders he briefly experienced, and he was soon transferred.
1945 CE	WWII ends, and many, many people die. Whether or not Axis leaders are barely saved by time travelers remains uncertain, but it's likely that at least Hitler's brain was saved and transplanted into a floating braincase. Ezeru exult in the creation of the atomic bomb.
1952 CE	Speaking of ezeru, this is the year that the hydrogen bomb is tested. The chrono-roaches take over key policy makers worldwide, nudging humanity towards nuclear war and greater atomic weapons. We systematically root them out one by one.
1957 CE	The beginning of the space age! The USSR launches Sputnik 1, and the race is on. Time traveling Europans attempt to sabotage and discourage space travel, hoping that this will lead to their species never being discovered.
1959 CE	World population reaches 3 billion. Even more people start to worry about overpopulation.
1960 CE	Seventeen different African nations achieve independence. Future warlords struggle in shifting paradoxes to see who controls what.
1962 CE	The Cuban Missile Crisis nearly gives the ezeru their wish of a global thermonuclear war.
1964 CE	The Civil Rights Act finally outlaws segregation in the United States – and don't even get me started about people who wish to change *that* piece of social advancement.
1967 CE	Ezeru attempt to capture and replace Paul McCartney, thus keeping the Beatles from traveling to India, in an inspired scheme to bring about nuclear war in the 1970s. The plot is accidentally foiled by low-paid temporary workers employed by a time machine manufacturing firm. We give them a medal when we sort out exactly what happened.
1973 CE	The Watergate scandal is manipulated by time travelers to protect Nixon; a surprising number of renegade volunteers travel through time to fix it back to normal.
1974 CE	In the jungles of Southeast Asia, a cluster of mutated Colony fungus

TIMELINE.

	colonizes multiple villages and begins to spread. TimeWatch calls in assistance from non-TimeWatch time travelers to identify and contain the source of the contagion.
1976 CE	The Ebola virus is accidentally brought from the future by an errant ezeru.
1977 CE	Elvis Presley ostensibly dies.
1980 CE	The death of John Lennon changes anticipated history, but no one at TimeWatch can prove that a time traveler engineered the murder, or even interfered. We're ordered to let it occur.
1983 CE	Tensions are high following the downing of Korean airliner Flight 007 by the Soviets, and a Soviet system hacked by ezeru almost launches nuclear missiles at the US when it misinterprets sunlight reflecting from clouds as rocket exhaust.
1986 CE	Europan-infected engineers approve launching the Challenger space shuttle in frigid temperatures, guaranteeing its destruction when an O-ring is too brittle to maintain a correct seal. The Europans are removed from play and time is rewound – and tragically, the non-infected engineers make the exact same decision.
1987 CE	Just as at the start of the Great Depression, self-interested time travelers work to get investment advice to their own ancestors before the stock market crashes.
1989 CE	We recruit the man who stood up to tanks in the Tiananmen Square Massacre in China.
1990 CE	The World Wide Web is invented, and the parasitic and intelligent language Te'Pk stands up and takes notice. Metaphorically speaking, I mean.
1991 CE	The Soviet Union disintegrates, and ezeru dart into the chaos to collect as many nuclear weapons and as much weapon-grade plutonium as they can manage.
1996 CE	Dolly the sheep becomes the first cloned mammal; instantly, a far future full of cloned humans rolls into place as potential reality. TimeWatch agents begin surreptitiously arranging for their own pre-mission clones, but the clones turn out to occasionally be resentful of the process. A very quiet and deadly war sneaks about

TIMELINE.

through the Citadel, with clone and original agent hunting each other and stealing each other's identities, and before long the shadow warfare leaks out into external missions as well. Not one person calls this "The Clone Wars."

1998 CE — Google is founded, leading to a future dystopia of massive privacy invasion and technological hostility. Cyborgs from a potential future escape before their parallel timeline collapses, entering true history and attempting to ensure their own survival.

1999 CE — World population reaches 6 billion. I'd say a robot uprising to winnow down the population starts to seem almost reasonable, but I'd be editorializing.

2000 CE — A tragic and deadly Y2K information crash is narrowly avoided by clocking out, heading back, and making sure engineers reprogram their systems with enough time to spare.

2001 CE — September 11 attacks on the US World Trade Center set off decades of paranoia, fear, and isolationist hatred. The War on Terror begins; TimeWatch finds itself dedicated to preventing worldwide terrorist attacks that use time machines.

2002 CE — Sophosaurs secretly take over American war propaganda, working to increase human fear and anxiety as a punishment for supplanting their own history with human history instead.

2004 CE — The Boxing Day tsunami in the Indian Ocean leaves 230,000 dead; TimeWatch and rebel groups recruit, while investigating if the earthquake was deliberately triggered. A small number of victims are swept through naturally occurring time rifts into other eras and parallel timelines.

2008 CE — Advances in AI and telephone technology herald the development of the tether.

We started seeing signs of intelligent AIs during this year, possibly transmitted backwards from the time period where they originated; specialized TimeWatch hackers begin trolling the Internet, eliminating the AI when it could be found.

2011 CE — Te'Pk discovers Internet memes and nearly colonizes the entire globe over a long weekend. Hackers trace the source before getting corrupted themselves, and TimeWatch heads in to eliminate

TIMELINE.

the source.

2013 CE — Mass surveillance by the NSA is exposed by Edward Snowden, and teenaged time travelers compete to acquire, destroy, or expose governmental secrets. Several of these would-be hackers become mature and sophisticated; those recruited into hostile rebel organizations become serious threats to TimeWatch's mission of preserving history.

2016 CE — Sophosaurs who are tasked with manipulating human culture reveal privately that they have been manipulating the 2016 presidential race. No one in TimeWatch is surprised.

FUTURE HISTORY

2021 CE — Undercover sophosaurs in Hollywood select a young comedian to create a seven-film series of an unintelligent, blundering, completely hilarious character that glorifies ignorance and rejects intellectualism. He ends up a smash hit, eroding popular culture just a little bit more. There's little visible effect, other than some smug and self-satisfied sophosaurs and a lot of movie tickets sold. Ironically, the quite intelligent comedian uncovers the truth and is recruited by TimeWatch.

2023 CE — Te'Pk manages to invade a new song of the world's most popular pop singer. Seventy million views later, the parasitic language has colonized a sizeable proportion of people in their teens and twenties. Reversing the colonization creates enough paradox to erase the TimeWatch team's identity from official records, although it's possible they survived.

2024 CE — An Alexandrian woman from the parallel timeline where Alexander the Great never died establishes herself as an American citizen and successfully runs for president, briefly bringing about a new golden age in American politics and international relations. Because she's from a parallel timeline, TimeWatch is forced to depose her. The debate this triggers within TimeWatch – the other candidates turn out to be reprehensible and bad for the country and world as a whole – results in multiple resignations and defections. Official response is harsh and autocratic.

2025 CE — A sophosaur privately reveals herself to a Nobel Prize–winning paleontologist, giving the appearance of striking up a friendship, then uses psychic powers to make herself invisible when he calls a press conference to reveal her to the world. The "invisible dino

TIMELINE.

friend" incident breaks him, and he spends the next 22 years hospitalized instead of exploring the fringes of science. Humanity loses out.

2026 CE — Underlying resentment from the Alexandrian Affair results in a TimeWatch civil war, with all-out warfare breaking out between agents who believe that the agency no longer has humanity's best interests in mind. All autochrons cease working for a period of several weeks in an attempt to quell the chaos, which strands or kills multiple agents.

Diplomatic efforts from TimeWatch's leadership work to rebuild goodwill between time agents, with mixed success. TimeWatch's mission as impartial defenders of humanity's true timeline is emphasized. Questions about how the true timeline is established are not answered, even when sophosaur agents are particularly vocal.

2029 CE — An authentically haunted house in central Mexico is declared "the most haunted site in the world" by paranormal investigators; TimeWatch investigation reveals that it's some sort of psychic magnet for disembodied time travelers, drawn there after experiencing chronal instability.

2032 CE — A 700-year-old immortal is unmasked in England. She runs for it, successfully assuming a new identity, but humanity becomes aware that it is apparently possible for the same person to live for centuries. The incident is eventually passed off as a hoax, but many suspicions and conspiracy theories remain.

2043 CE — India and Pakistan's short-lived nuclear exchange creates the Pakistan Nuclear Dead Zone. In some of the most innovative cyborg research to date, radiation-resistant assassination cyborgs are designed to carry on war where normal humans cannot.

2044 CE — Samantha Jane Underhill is accidentally created by government experiment, trapping a sociopathic off-the-charts genius in an ever-young small girl's body. She spends the next several hundred years performing more and more horrific experiments on human subjects while attempting to reverse her condition.

2045 CE — A terrorist sets off a dirty bomb in downtown Tokyo. If you thought security measures were autocratic and oppressive before, well, you have a lot to learn.

2047 CE — Another nuclear exchange occurs, this time emanating from

TIMELINE.

	North Korea. TimeWatch investigates – but if there's any trace of ezeru activity, we haven't found it yet.
2051 CE	Whole cities are designed to identify and track citizens. Everyone is identified by fingerprint and eye scan as they move through the city; railings track DNA, advertisements track gait and perform facial analysis, and a sophisticated AI keeps everything straight. Only private homes are partially isolated from surveillance. Things get tricky when time travelers arrive without being registered in the system or (worse!) being a duplicate of someone already in the system. In such a city, expect to spend as much time on the run as you do investigating, and remember that your autochron won't appear in any place that's being observed.
2058 CE	Advanced AI creates the first sentient hologram, allowing computers to talk to humans as (near) equals. This antecedent of tether technology serves as companions and robust information sources worldwide. Once infected with an offshoot of the Gloaming AI in 2066, they begin distributing knowledge in a method that systematically kills people or ruins their lives, revealing all learned secrets to crush peoples' reputations. Even after TimeWatch prevents the initial takeover, the popularity of sentient holograms takes a remarkable nosedive. We think there's some sort of paradoxical memory effect going on where people remember trauma that never actually happened, but no one is quite sure.
2061 CE	Irradiated cockroaches begin gaining sentience following widespread nuclear fallout across India and Pakistan. The roaches move in swarms and actively hunt larger prey. In most timelines intensive extermination reduces the threat; in a handful of timelines, these roaches eventually evolve into ezeru.
2065 CE	The Gloaming AI becomes the first artificial intelligence to reach full sentience; it quickly propels itself up into far superhuman intelligence and capability, taking innumerable steps to ensure its own success and survival. Eliminating humanity becomes its immediate priority. TimeWatch is able to intervene when it becomes clear that the Gloaming originates in the 31st century and used time travel to establish itself earlier. Despite stopping the AI from ever emerging, it somehow manages to duplicate itself in offline locations in preparation for later activation. Because time has been rewound, humanity never realizes how much danger it's in.
2068 CE	Military robots have become commonplace by 2050 or so, fighting

TIMELINE.

more battles than humans in both traditional and nontraditional theaters of engagement. This becomes a problem when the Gloaming AI re-emerges and establishes control, as normal security protocols are easily overridden by the AI. The slaughter is both innovative and remarkable.

2070 CE — Global warming floods coastlines around the world. Many cities either evacuate, abandoning their infrastructure to squatters and wildlife, or incorporate canals into their very nature. New York becomes known as New Venice after a remarkably successful conversion.

2072 CE — On the Day of Unveiling, a conspiracy theorist uses stolen anachronistic technology to strip away reptoid disguises during a political debate. Reptoids are exposed for the first time on national media, sending conspiracy groups into a frenzy and leading to vast purges of perfectly normal humans worldwide as hate groups try to exterminate "the alien menace in our midst." The use of futuristic technology means that TimeWatch has cause to reverse the unveiling, but now has known reptoid targets to confront.

2074 CE — A remnant of the Gloaming AI reactivates in a highly automated Japanese automobile-manufacturing facility. Thirty-six hours of chaos later, the majority of the 5,000 shift workers employed there have been transformed into cyborgs. TimeWatch is forced to step in to suppress the Gloaming before it further spreads.

2079 CE — The Louvre is burned to the ground during Parisian riots. Investigation suggests that the arson is deliberate and calculated; further investigation reveals a sophosaur agitator determined to destroy human art, using methods that ensure humans feel the loss keenly. TimeWatch intervenes.

2088 CE — Madagascar becomes infected with the Colony, declaring itself a part of world government despite the clear transition from human to sentient fungus of its citizens. Against accusations of racism and mass murder, the United Nations decides to treat the infestation as a fatal disease and sterilize the entire island with fire. TimeWatch struggles to prevent the infestation from taking hold, which requires tracking down Patient Zero.

2091 CE — The Gloaming AI re-emerges in new car systems, turning autonomous automobiles into murdering engines of death. We step in to flush the offline backup system that Gloaming re-emerged from,

THE THIRD ROBOT UPRISING, PARIS.

TIMELINE.

only to find that it has infected our tethers and autochrons. One massive technology purge later, we rely on backup methods to signal TimeWatch safe houses that we're in need of retrieval.

2101 CE — An overabundance of chronal leeches attach to anyone time traveling into or out of the Citadel, creating brief annoyance to anyone with a time machine who is thrown to an undesired time period. They're much more deadly when a pack of exiled leeches in the early 15th century descend on Central American cities and depopulate entire native civilizations. Surprisingly, some of those victims arrive in 2101 Nebraska.

2111 CE — Reptoids from 2111 devise a method of evading security when clocking into the Citadel, something that shouldn't even be possible. Worse, reptoids infiltrate the security teams responsible for confirming each agent's true and valid identity. Irreparable damage is done to the organization before a team of agents is able to uncover and unmask the conspiracy.

2142 CE — A TimeWatch mission gone wrong leads to world-wide paradox. Hundreds (perhaps thousands) of versions of the exact same TimeWatch agent appear across the globe, each with a different agenda. Alliances and rivalries between younger and older versions quickly spring up.

2160 CE — A known, one-way stable time rip allows transport from 22nd-century China back to 5.34 million years into the past. A rigid, autocratic government allows those who feel like they don't belong in modern society to take their chances and travel back in time. The government also uses it to dispose of known criminals. All travelers are sterilized before transport.

2212 CE — Meddling with Things Humanity Ought Not to Know produces the first uplifted superintelligent gorilla. He's far from the last, however.

2220 CE — The Vatican City State introduces its Ecclesiastical Infiltration Corps to stamp out heresy wherever it may be found. Heretics (actual or unintentional) take this rather badly.

2245 CE — There no easy way to know exactly when time travel is first invented; there are reports from the 1960s, the 1880s (H. G. Wells!), and numerous instances across the 20th and 21st centuries. With ancient standing stones and sophosaur interference, there are

A DUEL DURING THE PARADOX OF 2142.

TIMELINE.

even examples from preindustrial days, and let's not even get started on time rips. One thing is for sure, though. On 2245 CE, Dr. Leah Breen of New Zealand invents a time machine and uses it to systematically go back and sabotage earlier inventors. We don't necessarily know about everyone who came before her, but this is one of the first verified and consistent examples of a true time machine.

2248 CE — Time machines become regulated, then unregulated when someone goes back to change the law, then regulated again, and then unregulated as time travelers brazenly work to influence history in their favor. Chronal instability rises to worrying proportions and numerous lobbyists completely vanish from existence. No one minds.

2251 CE — Time tours come into vogue. Pick your historical event, and you can pay some eccentric entrepreneur with a malfunctioning time machine to take you to go see it.

For quite a while, many of these tours were tremendously unsafe; native fauna, hostile locals, and cumulative chronal instability added up to a lot of dead or stranded tourists. Worse, many tour groups accidentally (or sometimes purposely) sabotaged the actual historical events they had come to see. TimeWatch eventually stepped in to set up interdiction fields around the most popular, sensitive, or dangerous destinations.

2253 CE — The Erelim, fanatically religious time travelers, first make themselves known with a public announcement of their intent. The following day, their actions to inspire religious visions throughout history changes modern society into a highly devout theocracy. TimeWatch is called in to prevent their deliberate manipulation.

2259 CE — China launches the *Divine River*, the first manned spacecraft to Saturn and her moons. The ship returns four years later to international triumph. The captain's memoirs trigger renewed worldwide interest in interstellar exploration.

2266 CE — The Eternal Church of the Piercing Consciousness uses religion to send battalions of zealots off on one-way journeys into history, each group of the faithful armed with advanced technology and a religious mission to teach locals that time travel is real.

2281 CE — Scientists discover sentient life deep beneath Europa's ice, and it is far from pleased to have been discovered. Developing parasitic

TIMELINE.

and psychic manipulation, Europans travel to Earth to ensure that they never get discovered in the first place.

2297 CE — Newly industrialized Sierra Leone in West Africa becomes the hub of terrestrial space launches. While most spacecraft are built in orbit, we still need a method for getting parts and astronauts up to the space stations, and Western Africa develops substantial infrastructure to fill that need. Time travelers sabotaging spaceship launches remains a popular method of brutally eliminating a given country's dominance in the space race; TimeWatch spends quite a few missions detecting the saboteurs and stopping them before they can carry out their missions.

2299 CE — TimeWatch strikes a rough diplomatic agreement with a clan of sophosaurs using psychic abilities to manipulate world political events. For nine years, the duration of the truce, politics remains amazingly fair, kind, helpful, and hopeful. It doesn't last, but it's a nice respite – and it reveals how much mischief a psychic agitator can get up to when motivated.

2311 CE — The Chronal Purge. One inventor of a time machine is identified, someone quiet and secretive, and governmental assassins named "Paladins" are sent to kill all other time machine inventors before they ever have a chance to invent their devices. In doing so, the Paladins hope to stop reality and history from unraveling. It's thought by some that the Paladins were the antecedents to TimeWatch.

2320 CE — Wormholes are discovered and exploited, instantly killing everyone who attempts to utilize them for faster-than-light travel. Space travelers quickly stop using wormholes.

2333 CE — An accurate mathematical model of wormhole physics is developed by Dr. Katrina Sunderland and Dr. Halisi Kipyego, enabling consistent and moderately safe faster-than-light travel. Humanity begins to legitimately explore the stars.

2338 CE — Humanity reaches Alpha Centauri, using battle armor to settle several moons and colonize new territory. The settlers favor force over diplomacy with the native inhabitants, leading to lasting war. The Alpha Centauri settlements (nicknamed "Terra Nova") eventually separate from Earth-bound humanity, becoming in effect a new species of human. This pattern continues with other FTL expeditions and new planetary colonies.

TIMELINE.

2349 CE — The very definition of someone with more time and money than sense, a European billionaire named Elisabetta Horrell kidnaps cavemen and turns them into a personal cybernetic army. She deploys her personal army of chrome-magnons against business rivals and to take over small countries, hiding them elsewhere in time to avoid detection.

2368 CE — On the third FTL expedition, humanity discovers the alien race the k'horn and begins to wrestle with the now-universal knowledge that they aren't the only form of intelligent life. Of course, TimeWatch agents already know that, but it's a bit more of a shock for the general population.

2374 CE — A highly technological parallel timeline collapses, and time traveling cyborg refugees make their way into our own world in order to survive. TimeWatch chooses not to intervene (or maybe we try to and fail, I don't know. I've been told that around this time we're distracted by a chronal war with another time agency from a parallel timeline, but this is after my time so I've avoided the details).

Unlike some more hostile refugees, these cybes establish themselves as smart, strong, thoughtful individuals who make superb citizens of any country that will accept them. After they are compromised by a previously dormant strain of the Gloaming AI, they level new Singapore and start converting any animal they encounter. It takes a massive electromagnetic pulse for peacekeeping forces to regain control, and the surviving cybes live under stigma for the rest of their lives.

2380 CE — A diplomatic mission to greet an alien race of sentient gas called the reziki fails spectacularly. While the race agitates for our complete extinction, they do not yet possess FTL transportation. We withdraw and do not return.

2387 CE — Named after a similar location in ancient popular culture, the vast and tangled urban sprawl between Boston and Washington, DC (and encompassing Neo New York), is dubbed a Mega-City. Large sections become abandoned and forgotten as civil order breaks down, and toxic poisoning gives some members of the arcology low-grade psychic abilities. The Mega-City abruptly disappears after someone goes back and changes time, and TimeWatch has not yet been able to determine what got changed, when, in order to restore the correct timeline. Between you and me, I think at this point they're just trying to sweep the change under the rug.

TIMELINE.

2392 CE	The American Midwest becomes ground zero for a futuristic war of highly armed Japanese military commandos, sophosaurs, ezeru, and massive 50-meter-tall Gloaming AI cyborgs. There's nothing that TimeWatch can initially do to hide this chronal catastrophe; agents slowly peel back the sources of the conflict in the hopes of preventing it, and meanwhile, waves of devastation ripple through the world.
2396 CE	With sizeable portions of North America devastated by war, a team of TimeWatch agents succeeds at erasing the causes of the chronal war. All combatants vanish and time reknits itself as if the war never occurred – except everyone still remembers it. This becomes a sort of shared delusion, a disturbing experience that most people who lived through it just don't discuss.
2412 CE	New breakthroughs in genetics lead to near-perfect cloning techniques. TimeWatch quickly adopts these for black market use by agents concerned about particularly deadly missions.
2430 CE	Experimentation with parallel realities uncovers a distant world made of living sound, where exposure to native creatures leaves humans sobbing with the beauty of the music their very life produces.
2452 CE	Geneticist Dr. Dansky Cordova begins his breeding program of cryptids, systematically creating all the mythical monsters known throughout history. He and other bioengineers like him take great delight in sending them back in time to create conspiracy theories and start legends. He uses one-way technology and great skill to make sure we can't trace them back to him – and then he brags about it in the future equivalent of social media.
2470 CE	A plague sweeps out of Indonesia and spreads worldwide before it can be stopped. Seventy percent of Earth-bound humanity dies; technology suffers a similar dark age, with the knowledge-keepers dying and few people left to service and maintain the machines. Nonhuman inhabitants of Earth vie to control remaining humanity. Wars, either small or large (and partially carried out by killer robots), rage for the next several centuries. A small number of incredibly wealthy individuals survive, primarily in floating cities or space stations.
2527 CE	The radioactive deserts of Australia breed their own style of horrors. A tribe of once-human raiders ride out of the wastes to raid

TIMELINE.

the rich and supposedly secure coastal cities around the continent; thousands of the raiders then take to the sea, pillaging shipping and making forays into Southeast Asia.

2536 CE — Amundscott, Antarctica, is established as a refuge from plague, global warming, and radioactive fallout.

2722 CE — Advanced humanity returns to Earth, using super-science to clean the oceans and atmosphere. Over the next 150 years, humanity is dragged back from the brink of extinction into a new renaissance of learning, education, and rebuilding. The First Matriarchy establishes itself in an empire that spans the globe, with a capital in the heart of the Congo.

2866 CE — Newly educated citizens rise up after the first matriarch transcends her body in favor of the Imperial Braincase. The First Matriarchy War.

2950 CE — The Second Matriarchy rules for almost 300 years, pacifying dissident groups in China and expanding throughout Asia and Eastern Europe through both precise force and extremely sophisticated psychographic reprogramming. Unlike the First Matriarchy eighty years before, the Second Matriarchy cannot be said to be a time of peace and prosperity; but the people who aren't exterminated are well fed, and in its later years the draconian methods used to enforce peace are relaxed in favor of advanced philosophy and universal education. At the end of the Matriarchy, when the wars begin to rage for independence, the soldiers are the best-educated soldiers in history.

3220 CE — The Yellowstone Caldera blows. Bye-bye, North America.

Sophosaurs everywhere time travel forwards to this point, presumably just to thumb their collective noses at the survivors; then they clock out for the last time, presumably seeking a more hospitable period of history to settle.

3221 CE — We get our own mini ice age as the Yellowstone supervolcano shoots massive ash into the heavens. Some of this is cleaned up with new technology from off-world industries, but there's worldwide famine as global temperatures drop abruptly. It's an extinction-level event, and humanity struggles to get as many people as possible out to other planets. For everyone else, there's struggle – and the unexpected nuclear wars that break out over scarce resources.

TIMELINE.

The balance of power in the world changes abruptly; the next few hundred years are not at all pretty, and it takes almost a thousand years before temperatures are back to normal. On the plus side, people stop worrying about global warming. It's believed that the supervolcano was deliberately triggered by sophosaur science.

3230 CE — TimeWatch is officially founded.

JOURNAL OF EDWARD PLANTAGENET.

A.K.A. KING EDWARD V OF ENGLAND, BORN 1470 CE.

EDWARD V.
2 NOVEMBER 1470 – 1483

KING OF ENGLAND 9 APRIL 1483 – 26 JUNE 1483

EDWARD V.

2317 CE, SEPTEMBER 23
Mars Colony Beta.

Successful landing at initial destination. Mars Colony Beta is just as crowded as I remember from my last mission here; they've really outgrown the second dome. And it's noisy! Why is the 25th century so loud everywhere you go? I keep thinking that jetcars would make the city quieter, but no.

Sotheby's believed my credentials as the personal assistant to a wealthy buyer who wanted to remain anonymous, and allowed me in to see the paintings that were up for auction.

St. Francis Preaching to the Birds definitely fits Caravaggio's later style: a sacred subject depicted with attention to the material. The saint's bare feet are dirty. I'm not sure about the sincerity of Caravaggio's faith, but I can't doubt his skill. It's a truly magnificent painting.

If he was actually the one who painted it, of course. I suppose that it could be an excellent forgery, or it could actually be a previously unknown painting by the real Caravaggio in this timeline, which is what all of the catalogs and news reports are saying about it. But most likely, it was actually painted by Caravaggio in another timeline, and brought into this one by a thief or fraudster, just as they did with those Vermeers in the early 20th century. So I'll need to get my hands on it and bring it to our expert.

The only trouble is that the starting bid is 500 million standard solar credits, and I'm sure it's going to go much higher. I'm going to need more money.

2250 CE
Boston.

Set up investment portfolio with my initial budget from TimeWatch. Late 24th-century interest should help me get enough to buy the Caravaggio without having to draw too much on TimeWatch funds.

2317 CE, SEPTEMBER 24
Mars Colony Beta.

I got it! *St. Francis Preaching to the Birds* is mine. Well, TimeWatch's. It was a rather tight competition, and for a little while I thought that one of the Mars Colony Alpha mining CEOs (or, more precisely, her representative) was going to outbid me, but I managed to get it.

I took the painting to Dr. Patel, and she said that it is undoubtedly a late Caravaggio. The brushstrokes match the techniques he was using near the end of his life, and in some cases those techniques are even more pronounced. I admit that I did not quite follow all of Dr. Patel's discussion of painting techniques, but the important part is that the brushstrokes match Caravaggio's later style.

However, the choice of colors is slightly different from Caravaggio's usual palette: this painting is done in darker tones, with fewer of the bright highlights that Caravaggio was accustomed to using. Perhaps he was experimenting with different color techniques as well, suggested Dr. Patel?

I don't know yet if any of this information is significant to any larger pattern, but it all seems to confirm our theory that it's been brought in from another timeline, and it gives me some concrete clues that we can use to identify other Caravaggios from the same timeline.

«later»

I asked Sotheby's how they got the painting, and they said that it was sold to them by an Italian woman who had had it in her family for centuries. She had all of the documentation to prove it: photographs, letters, etc. Which doesn't really mean anything, because it's easy to leap about in time and produce the right kind of letters, legal documents, and photographs. I asked to see the documentation, and just as I expected, the photographs showed that the seller bore a remarkable resemblance to her mother, grandmother, and great-grandmother – she leaped about in time to create the proof she'd need.

I ran the images through TimeWatch's databases, but the face doesn't match any of our known time criminals.

If we have another timeline-hopping art thief, I know one place I can go to get more information, but I'd really rather not. I'm going to exhaust all other possibilities before I go *there*.

2122 CE, AUGUST
Milan, Italy.

Well, I've exhausted all other possibilities. I thought I could trace the locations where the thief had photographed herself with the painting, or perhaps get information on some of the lawyers who had helped draw up the legal documents.

No luck anywhere. I've visited half-a-dozen lawyers in half-a-dozen decades, and even figured out enough 22nd-century Italian law to be able to talk intelligently to them, but none of them could give me any worthwhile information other than yes, they'd met her. She's covered her tracks well.

I really don't want to have to do this, but I don't have any other choice.

I have to go talk to Richard.

1956 CE, MAY 4
Greenwich Village, New York.

Richard's apartment in Greenwich Village is just as small as I had remembered, and even more shabby. There is a drunkard on the front steps and no lock on the front door of the building.

Richard is just as I had remembered, too – black turtleneck, scruffy attempt at a beard, endlessly smoking cigarettes and talking about poetry. And he's working as a bricklayer, of all things! When I said that he was probably the highest-born and best-educated bricklayer in the world, he started lecturing me about the nobility of labor and the unity of the proletariat. How can he be in the proletariat? He's the son of a king!

I really hope he gets over Communism soon.

Bricklaying isn't making him enough money, either. He left one of the kitchen cupboards open, and I could see that there was hardly any food in the place.

Fortunately, once he stopped talking about the proletariat he was actually willing to have a conversation. Unfortunately, he thought it was absolutely hilarious that I needed his help on a TimeWatch case, and tried to get me to promise all kinds of things in exchange for his information. I had to remind him that TimeWatch had already been very generous, and that his giving us information on the shadier sort of time traveler was just upholding his end of the bargain.

After several more rounds of negotiation, and several more rounds of gloating that TimeWatch was asking *him* for a favor, Richard finally gave me what I needed: the name of the woman in the picture, and the chronal coordinates where I can find her.

Who has, in fact, been hanging about in time traveler bars talking about the fortune she's made in art that she's brought from another timeline – paintings, jewelry, even gold-plated statues. Her name is Elena Montano, she's got an unlicensed Tempus 4500 travel device, and she tends to make her entry into this timeline via her family's estate in Florence.

EDWARD V.

1956 CE, MAY 12
Greenwich Village, New York.

Leaped into Richard's apartment when he wasn't there and hid some money in the pocket of his coat so that when he finds it, he'll think he put it there himself and forgot about it.

He's a wastrel, but he's my brother, and I'm going to take care of him.

1827 CE
Villa Montano, Florence, Italy.

I arrived at Villa Montano a few hours before the chronal coordinates that Richard gave me so that I can set up a trap for the thief. I'll turn on the tether's recording function so that I can make sure to get all of the information.

Begin tether recording.

[scuffling noise]

"Elena Montano, you are under arrest."

[muffled cursing] "Hey! That's my statue! Take your filthy hands off it! And that's my Tempus! Give me back my Tempus!" [more scuffling sounds] [pause] [more quietly] "So. Are you going to kill me?"

"What? Of course not. I said that you were under arrest. You're captured, disarmed, and not fighting back. You haven't tried to hurt me, and my sources inform me that you haven't hurt anyone else. As long as all of that stays true, I will do you no harm."

[groan] "TimeWatch. Who else would be so honorable?"

"That's right. And, really, you don't need to make it sound like an insult."

[snort]

"The statue. Where did you get it?"

"Right here."

"You know what I mean."

"I told you – I got it here! From this house! Just, you know, a couple timelines to the west. You've got my Tempus – you can take the chronal coordinates from there."

"Oh, I will. But I wanted to give you a chance to tell me, so that it will go easier for you."

"Frickin' TimeWatch. What, you didn't bring a bad cop with you to give some decent threats while you're being all good cop and reasonable?"

"I just want to ask you some questions. I don't see what you gain by resisting. You know I'm going to arrest you anyway."

[sigh] "Fine. Whatever."

"I know you're not a violent criminal, Ms. Montano. You're just looking for profit, isn't that right?"

[sigh] "Yeah. I used to be doing a good business – made a fortune on the stuff I took from the Gardner! But it's getting too crowded in this timeline. Everyone and his uncle's shuffling art around. You can't hit a museum fast enough before some other time traveler's hopped in ahead of you. Last month I had this Picasso stolen right out from under me! *Le pigeon aux petits pois*. I know I could've gotten billions for it in the right market in the right century. But no, someone else got there first. That's when I gave up on this timeline and started looking for others. You know, artists make different things in every timeline – in this one they have a happier childhood, and in that one they have a tragic love affair, in this one they live longer, in that one they just feel like painting in red that day instead of blue. Any little thing can make their art different. But you've still got an authentic piece by that artist that any expert will certify."

"Like the Caravaggio *St. Francis*?"

"Yeah. Like that. Caravaggio painted it. Just, you know, not this Caravaggio. Same timeline that I got the statue from. I have to tell you – this timeline is fabulous. Tons of paintings. Gold-plated statues everywhere! You think this one's nice? You should've seen the one I took from the papal apartments –"

"You stole from the *pope*?"

[laughter] "What? He could spare it. He had a ton of 'em."

"Where did you sell that one?"

"2012. Super easy to slip some more gold into the market there."

"And the Caravaggio? Where did you get that?"

"I told you, I got it here. 1622." [laughter] "My ancestors never even got it. I took it from the courier as he was bringing it to the villa."

"That's all the information I need, Ms. Montano."

«later»

Elena Montano is brave; I will give her that much. Even when she thought I was going to kill her, she showed no fear. But she is also a criminal, and I've sent her back to TimeWatch to face justice for her crimes.

I hopped back to 2317 so that I could pick up the painting, then over to the coordinates that Montano gave me. She was telling the truth: the villa belongs to her family, and they're extremely wealthy. The villa is even larger in this timeline than in the prime.

I'll leap in to put the statue back, MEM-tag the courier, then take the courier's place and deliver *St. Francis*. They'll never know that the statue and painting were ever gone. Case closed.

1622 CE, NOVEMBER 25
Villa Montano, Florence, Italy.

Well, that took longer than I expected. I still don't know what to make of everything I've heard, but I do know that this mission is not over after all.

After replacing the statue, I leaped a few hours earlier so that I could enter Villa Montano as the courier delivering the Caravaggio. One of the servants let me in, and directed me to the family chapel. The building was even more opulent than I had realized: the floors are marble, the tapestries on the walls have gold threads in them, and there are more gold-plated statues throughout the villa. Even the chapel is full of gold: a gold altar service, gold candlesticks, and real gold halos on all of the statues.

I hung the Caravaggio in the place where I was instructed, and then paused for a moment to pray. That is when two of the ladies of the house came in to admire the painting. As soon as I heard what they were saying, I forgot about my prayers and just kept my head bowed so that I could listen.

Maria Montano – the mother – wondered if Caravaggio would be willing to take another commission for a similar painting. That meant that Caravaggio was still alive in this timeline, where according to the tether he died in 1610. That explains the slight differences in style: he grew as an artist as he aged. The daughter, Giovanna, talked a bit about the financial arrangements, and finished by saying that she would speak to the alchemist to see if it was possible.

Alchemist? Do people in this timeline consult alchemists the way some people consult astrologers, I wondered: asking them to see if a particular decision would be auspicious?

No. That wasn't it at all. As they talked, it became clear that Giovanna wasn't talking about the alchemists as if they were astrologers, but as if they were banks. The Montanos were going to get some gold made.

Of course! That is why there is gold everywhere. In this timeline, alchemists can actually create gold. Who gave them that kind of technology, and when?

EDWARD V.

I need to find an alchemist. And a history book.

1622 CE, NOVEMBER 26
Florence.

Now that I know what to look for, I can see how the addition of gold has changed the city. There are golden statues at the entry of every villa, gold threads in the clothing of the rich merchants. Gold seems to be the only way of showing your status, and those who have it show it wherever they can.

But the secret of creating gold clearly isn't open to everyone. There is poverty everywhere – half-a-dozen beggars grabbed my feet as I walked over the Ponte Vecchio, and I heard the shouts of I don't know how many more. I wish I could help them all, but there are just too many.

It was easy to find an alchemist's shop, but hard to get in. There are several large guards at the door (with gold inlay on their helmets, of course), and there is a long line. While I waited, I surreptitiously searched the tether for more information on Caravaggio. It told me that in the prime timeline, he died in 1610, after a long illness... which some suspect to be lead poisoning.

Oh, it all makes sense! Lead is what the alchemists always wanted to turn into gold. If they actually could do that, lead would never be used for anything as mundane as paint. Caravaggio wouldn't have come into contact with enough lead to have been sickened by it. So here he is, twelve years after he should have died, still alive and well and painting. I suspect that the absence of lead in paint also explains the differences in paint color that Dr. Patel noticed.

It was easier than I expected to find lead: coins in Florence are made of lead. Being able to turn lead into gold has given the base metal some value of its own. So I collected a few coins, and went back to the shop to wait. And wait. And wait.

Several hours later, I got in. The alchemist's shop was entirely covered in gold: gold candlesticks, gold desk, gold chairs. It was clearly meant to dazzle and impress, and it did its job well. The alchemist himself didn't register as being out of his proper time, and neither did any of his tools, but the design of his equipment was very clearly not seventeenth century. He was very secretive about his practice, but couldn't resist mentioning the Philosopher's Stone as he worked.

The Philosopher's Stone is a myth! Everyone knows that. But someone has given it to this timeline.

EDWARD V.

1622 CE, NOVEMBER 27
Naples.

After I'd seen alchemy in action, I went to find out more about its origins. Italy has the best universities in Europe in this timeline as well as my own, so I hopped over to the one that was strongest in natural philosophy.

It was easy enough to pretend to be a new student from England and blend in with the other students – the more truth you can tell, the easier your cover story is – and tried to find a lecture on the history of alchemy.

For some reason, the other students thought that I was absolutely hilarious.

Once I actually got into the lecture on the history of alchemy, I found out. Alchemy is so closely guarded that nobody can just walk into a lecture the way they can on other areas of natural philosophy. And also, alchemy started in England. Apparently the best place to study alchemy is at Oxford. So it would make no sense for an English student to come all the way to Italy.

I'm gratified that everyone sees England as an advanced center of learning, but being laughed at still stung a bit.

The open lectures don't discuss any of the actual technicalities of alchemy, just the history, but that was enough. Apparently the first to discover the Philosopher's Stone was the scholar Robert of Chester, who lived and worked in London around 1150.

I have to go back to London?

1150 CE, AUGUST 21
London.

I've been to Mars and I've been to ancient Rome and I've been to the literal end of time, but none of those places has been so strange to me as my own city 300 years before my birth.

Some of the streets almost look the same, but they seem wider because the buildings haven't crowded in as much. There are more gardens between the houses, more space for animals to graze, and the whole north side of the city is a broad pasture with mill wheels turning in the streams. The great bridge over the Thames is in the same place, but it's wood, not stone. The streets still echo with the same city shouts and peddlers' cries, but if I turn off the tether I can't understand them – both English and French are too different here.

The White Tower looks taller, newer, cleaner. The walls have sharper edges – it's been less than a century since the Conqueror built it. But it's all alone there on the hill. When people talk about "the Tower" they only mean the one castle. None of the other towers have been built yet.

The Garden Tower isn't there at all.

At least it wasn't as greatly changed as Florence. I can still feel that I'm out of my home timeline, but I'm closer to the branch point. London looks exactly as it should at this time, but it all looks wrong. I want to stay, but I want to go home.

I have to get through this quickly.

«later»

Harmondsworth Priory is much farther from the city than I realized. It looks more like a manor than a monastery, with a large house at the center surrounded by farms and fields.

I found Robert of Chester out in the meadows, near the beehives. He was surprisingly friendly and willing to talk to me. He isn't a time traveler; he's local to this timeline. He's highly intelligent and highly educated – probably one of only four or five people in England at this time who can read Arabic. That is how he was able to learn so much about mathematics and alchemy: he spent several years in Spain studying and translating texts from Arabic into Latin. It was in those texts that he discovered the secret of the Philosopher's Stone.

If Robert himself isn't the time traveler, then one of his collaborators must have been. Sure enough, when I asked, he said that he'd gotten a lot of help from a man named Brother William, whom he met in Toledo six years ago, and who always happened to be the one who translated the most interesting texts about alchemy.

That has to be the time traveler. How easy would it be for him to hand Robert a "previously unknown" book that actually had future tech in it?

Brother William occasionally visits Robert here – he finds the beehives peaceful – and they talk about alchemy, but Robert isn't sure where William goes between those visits. He said that the last of those visits was about a fortnight ago. I'll plant some listening devices and see what they're talking about.

1150 CE, AUGUST 6
London.

Planted surveillance bugs in the beehives. That should do the trick.

EDWARD V.

1150 CE, AUGUST 8
London.

Listened to the conversation between Robert and William. William was definitely feeding Robert information about nuclear transmutation. He's the time traveler. But there was something else in the surveillance audio. I could hear a buzz under Brother William's words every time he talked. The noise from the beehive nearly masked it, but I could adjust the sound enough so that I could hear that the buzzing wasn't just the bees. William is an ezeru. No wonder he likes visiting Robert near the beehives.

Of course the ezeru would be behind a plot like this! They would want to decrease the amount of lead in the world because lead shields against radiation. I'm glad to have figured out the answer, but it sickens me to think of the ezeru in London. In my city!

Robert said that he first met William in 1144, when they were working in Toledo. That's where I need to go if I want to stop this plot for good.

But to do that, I need backup. And I need something that can take out an ezeru.

«later»

Heard back from HQ. Dr. Rosario's sending some of her latest sub-acoustic modulators. They're still experimental, but they should be able to counteract the ezeru's sonic attacks. Even better, HQ is sending Kate Symond and Kim Jae. Jae thinks better on his feet than almost any other agent I know, and Kate is incredibly determined. I'm glad she's back on active duty, and I know she'll always have my back. But I worry that she might try to keep too close to my back. To her, I'm still the child she rescued, even though I've been a full agent for years now.

1144 CE, FEBRUARY 17
Toledo, Spain.

Kate and Jae showed up right on schedule with the sub-acoustic modulators. Planning went well; Jae can take any plan and run with it. Kate tried to get me to stay away from the fight, just as I thought she would. But I won't ask anyone else to take a risk that I'm not willing to take myself. Anyway, this started out as my mission, and I'll see it through.

We scouted the cliffs and ravines near the city. We'll lure the ezeru to one of them, then trigger a landslide with the sub-acoustic modulators. That should be enough to crush it, and still have it far enough away from the city so there won't be any civilian casualties or property damage.

«later»

I found Robert of Chester in the cathedral library, working with a group of other scholars on one of their translations. Robert told me that he expected Brother William to return later that day, and he'd send him out to me.

Oh. That's probably why he was so friendly in 1150: he recognized me from six years before. I should really be more careful about that. Being in London must have thrown me off more than I realized – I know better than to make a slip like that.

1144 CE, FEBRUARY 18
Toledo.

We won. That's all that matters. We won.

The first part went exactly according to plan. Kate, Jae, and I stationed ourselves at the edge of the cliff and set our sub-acoustic modulators to the proper frequency. As soon as Brother William appeared at the city gates, we activated the modulators. The psychic field that made it look human was still active, but when the ezeru heard our modulators, it reared up and waved its arms just as a cockroach would.

We tried to steer the ezeru towards the cliff, and we thought we were well hidden, but somehow it spotted the others and charged right towards them. I dived forward to blast it, and I got off a good shot or two that drew it away.

Then it sprayed me.

There was horrible slime everywhere, all over my face and body. I could feel it pressing in, trying to get into my thoughts. My skin went numb.

I couldn't breathe. I couldn't breathe. I was a child again with a pillow being pressed over my face.

But I could still hear Kate shouting "Now!"

So I did.

I heard the frequency change, and I felt the earth start to rumble as the landslide crushed down over the ezeru.

As soon as it was done, the pressure lifted from my mind.

EDWARD V.

I pushed the slime away from my face, and Kate helped me up. I wanted to be able to thank her, but I couldn't talk, not for a long time.

Jae looked like he wanted to ask what was going on, but mercifully, he didn't. Kate didn't need to ask. She knew.

She stayed for a few minutes after Jae went back to HQ, and apologized that she couldn't stay longer, but she had another investigation that she needed to get back to. I hadn't realized until then how tired she looked. I offered to help – I wanted to think about something else, anything else! But she said no, she didn't need me. Which means that it's either one of her private investigations, or that she thinks it's too dangerous to involve me in, or both. I wish she'd stop being so overprotective.

But I'm glad she was there.

1956 CE, MAY 15
Greenwich Village, New York.

HQ says that everything is resolved: the other timeline has entirely collapsed. I must have sounded fine when I was making my report, because they didn't comment.

Case closed – really, this time.

Except that last night I woke up from a nightmare where I couldn't breathe. And the night before that. And the night before that.

So here I am.

I don't know if Richard will let me in, but I'm going to try anyway. I need to talk to my brother.

end

Veduta dell'ingresso alla Villa Montano

THE MONTANO VILLA WAS SPECTACULAR IN ITS DAY.

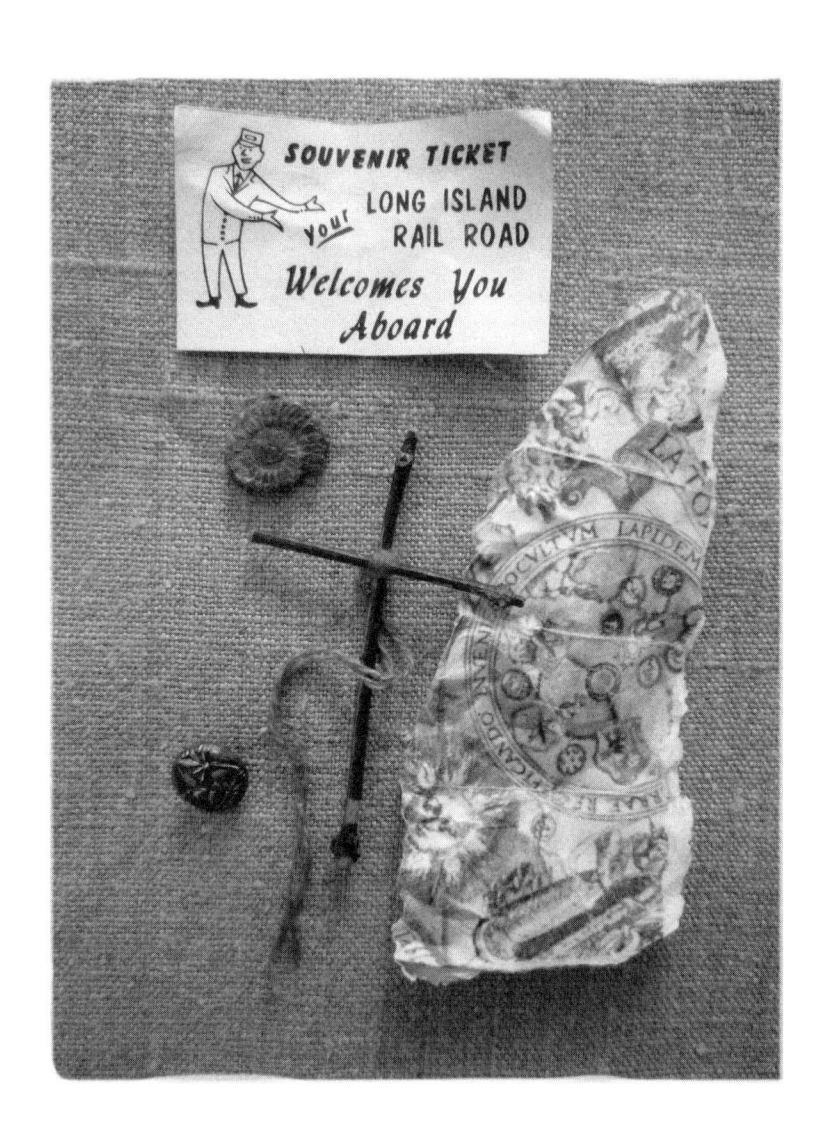

EDWARD V.

JOURNAL OF AMBROSE BIERCE.

AMBROSE BIERCE.
24 JUNE 1842 –

SOLDIER, JOURNALIST AND AUTHOR OF
"AN OCCURRENCE AT OWL CREEK BRIDGE"

AMBROSE BIERCE.

1913 CE, DECEMBER 26.

As to me, I leave here tomorrow for an unknown destination. I am an old man, and I have already seen my share of adventure and heartache. But what awaits is too intriguing to dismiss. The future, the past. Everything. Enough to intrigue even an old man. Yes, I have been invited to join some holy order – or perhaps social club? – called TimeWatch.

My friends, acquaintances, and yes, admirers, will wonder where I have gone. I may send a letter or two before we are away, if only to stir the pot. The scandal it will cause is delicious, I admit it.

General Villa is safe, of course. My new companions assure me that battles greater still than Tierra Blanca await him, though they are reticent to speak of his surely unending friendship with the United States. Regardless, his survival at Tierra Blanca is evidently necessary to some future history.

The general is in more than enough danger as it is, but my companions tell me that the assassins we had ferreted out at Tierra Blanca were not of this age or world: refugee activists from a distant-future Porfiriato, seeking to rebuild what they saw as a better, stronger Mexico! Having seen the way Díaz preyed upon his people, I cannot imagine their lost future being better than this; regardless, their well-meaning interference should come at the cost of all human existence.

My new compatriots seem unmoved by the evidently apocalyptic scale of the consequences of the very real possibility of our failure. Instead, they whisper among themselves of others – fellow time travelers? – who never arrived as expected, their mysterious time machines malfunctioning and depositing them God only knows when. Though they do not say it, I suspect my recruitment was more panicked improvisation than any grand plan to use my privileged position of observation with the general to gain closer access to him.

My friends assure me that we have won the day, but I cannot help but fear that even now we play a game according to someone else's strategy.

But perhaps there is time enough to explore it all: to understand. Time enough indeed!

end

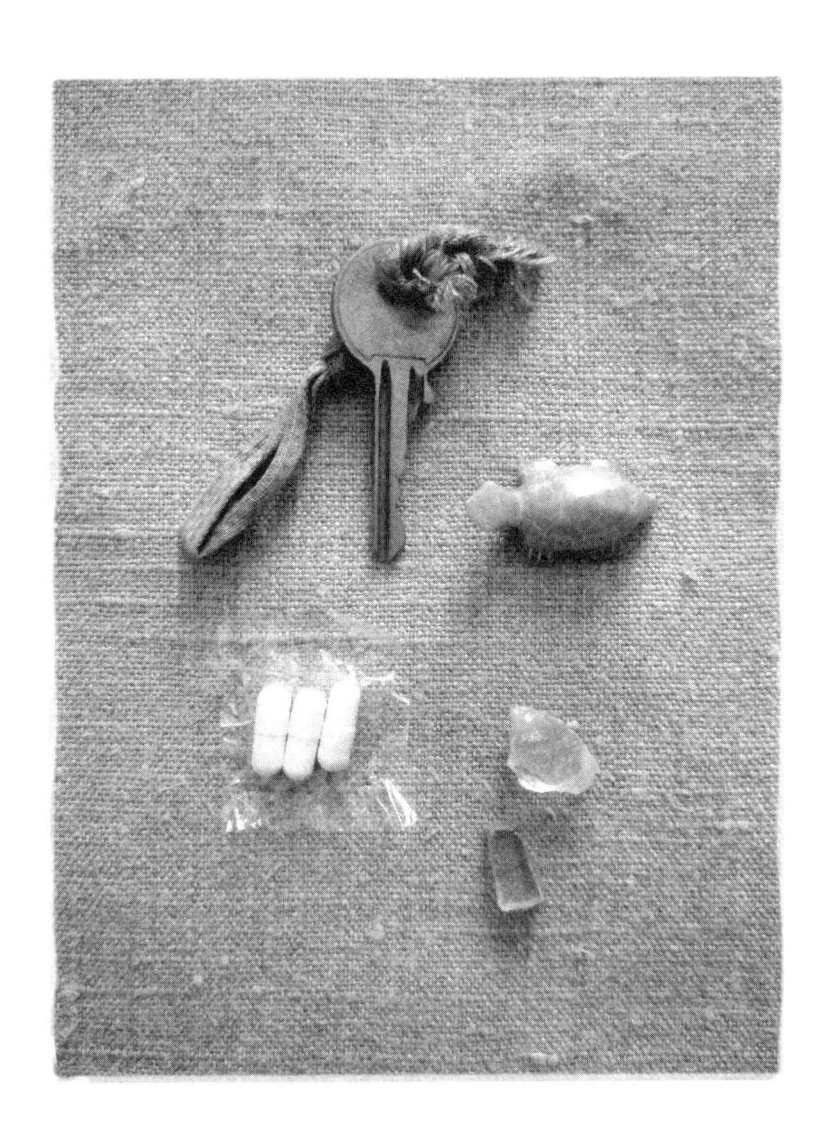

AMBROSE BIERCE.

REPORT FROM AGENT SNOW

AGENT SNOW.

AGENT SNOW.

REPORT 1. TIME STAMP:[1903] AGENT ID:[SNOW].

Snow, signing in for a pre-mission thought-log submission for TimeWatch's Psychological Division. I understand that these check-ins are a part of my probation period, and I will answer as honestly as I know how.

 The greatest challenge I face is feeling like I don't fit in with the other agents. TimeWatch has provided me with all of the proper equipment to help me cope with any physical changes or problems that I may be experiencing due to time travel, but they cannot force the team to like me . . . Everyone I knew from my timeline is gone, and even though I know my team is sympathetic to whatever loss that entails, I can't seem to connect with them in any real way. My timeline doesn't exist anymore. What good are friends if they can be erased at a moment's notice?

 My heart is heavy with the loss of the friends and family I left in my weather-torn timeline. I think about it often. I think it is what drives me to work with TimeWatch. I saw, firsthand, the devastating effects global warming can have on the planet and its inhabitants. The summer heat on Earth was unbearable, and the only *relief* would come from huge dust storms that blotted out the sun and covered the city for days at a time. When winter came it came abruptly, dropping below freezing for months at a time without wavering.

 It was no wonder humans were so eager to abandon Earth for the quiet blanket of space. Our everyday life was dominated by the fight for food, water, and shelter. The little comforts went first, and when all we had left to do was hope, humanity left Earth and took to the stars . . . but we couldn't all go. I was one of the lucky few to leave Earth, and I was the only one to leave that timeline. I owe everything to TimeWatch for recruiting me.

 I still remember when Amar came to see me in the engine room of the *Eta Draconis*, a space station that housed almost 1 million people. One-third of Earth's remaining population . . . I recognized him as an outsider almost immediately. (When you are used to the limits of space station textiles, blue fabric tends to stand out.) The interview was brief: he walked up to the engine core that I had built and asked me what I was thinking about. I trusted him and responded honestly, "I am thinking about how I can help them. I never stop thinking about how I could have helped them." My answer seemed to be good enough for him. I was recruited from the *Eta Draconis*' engine room just before my timeline was "corrected."

 Sometimes I wonder what would have happened if I had stayed in my timeline and used my engineering skills to help restore the planet instead of abandoning it and running to the stars. Even now, drifting through time, I can't help but see signs

AGENT SNOW.

of what happened to cause the crisis in my timeline: the flippant political responses to global warming as a credible threat in 2013, the excessive amount of resources spent on 2250s' space exploration and xeno-programs, the botched diplomatic mission to greet the reziki in 2380. So much was lost because we were too arrogant to change before it was too late...

– Agent Snow

REPORT 2. TIME STAMP:[1903] AGENT ID:[SNOW].

I was recently reassigned to a 1903 case. I was asked to deliver alternate plans for Orville and Wilbur Wright's first successful airplane, swapping their designs for blueprints provided by TimeWatch HQ. I was able to switch the plans easily, but when I looked at the timeline results, this mission seemed to have altered the timeline dramatically. (I'm sure TimeWatch is aware of the shift.)

Without the advent of heavy aircraft, most of Earth's technological advances have become focused on biological and geological developments. Humans are not contributing to global warming in this new timeline; they appear to focus on agriculture and mining techniques that work in harmony with nature and the environment. Even ground transportation seems to be faster and smoother than ever! (Can't say I even miss the old clunky way of getting around.) The air is cleaner, and there seem to be more expansive nature preserves.

Although the future of this altered timelines seems to be green-friendly, there is now a lack of xeno-diversity from contact period on and Earth's political structures appear to be more fragile than ever before. Earth is now insular, and only communications have been shot into space; no human has set foot on anything so close as the moon. It seems to me that whatever hegemonic forces were holding the planet together in my timeline never developed here.

I feel hopeful, despite the obstacles inherent in such political conflicts. TimeWatch HQ must know best, right? This must be better than the other outcomes...

– Agent Snow

REPORT 3. TIME STAMP:[MISSING] AGENT ID:[SNOW].

I must keep this brief and omit my time stamp for I fear that I may be attacked again.

I do not understand what forces are at work here, but I have just narrowly escaped an altercation with fellow TimeWatch agents. They attempted to neutralize me in 1903 just after I checked in with HQ to report my mission status, but I have avoided them for now.

I saw them coming, but there was nothing I could do. We were in the middle of an open field used for failed test flights with gigantic rolling hills leading down to a forest tree line. When I saw Amar and the others I waved, but they did not return the gesture. Instead, several of them leveled their weapons at me. Panicked and desperate I looked to Amar for support, but he merely shook his head at me. Getting to the tree line was my only hope of survival, so I ran...

I was deaf to everything but the sound of my rhythmic panting and heart pounding heavily in my chest. I ran for what seemed like hours. Fatigued from sprinting for so long I lost my footing and fell. To escape the agents I threw my body down the hill and began rolling furiously toward the tree line as fast as possible. When I reached the tree line I was dizzy and disoriented, but knew I was safe. I have always been better at hiding than Amar was at hunting. My team shot their weapons futilely into the forest, and I disappeared into the thicket without a trace.

I'm guessing that something about the Wright brothers' mission has gone sour, but I maintain my innocence. The other agents would not hear my case, but I will continue to report to HQ in hopes that I will receive a response and be allowed to clear my name. These reports will surely give HQ what they need to resolve this.

– Agent Snow

REPORT 4. TIME STAMP:[MISSING] AGENT ID:[MISSING].

Despite my attempts to initiate contact and clear my name, I have not received any communication from TimeWatch HQ since the initial altercation in 1903. I keep talking, but no one is listening! I'm all alone out here, dammit!

In the absence of answers, I have been pursuing the agent who sent me what I now believe to have been a false mission. Somehow the agent was able to spoof HQ's authorization codes and knew my private key encoder and agent ID. I don't know why they would do this, but I will find out who caused this chaos.

And since my co-agents at TimeWatch are relentlessly pursuing me, I have been forced to anonymously post these entries to the TimeWatch servers. This is in no way an admission of guilt, and I will continue to sign these updates as "Agent Snow," but I don't know who to trust, and until I can prove that I was set up, I will have to continue to operate without the approval of TimeWatch... and without the watchful eye of HQ on my activities.

On the off chance that these messages are being intercepted, I will be attempting to make contact with the next team of agents sent after me. I will not agree to be taken into custody (or killed!), but I am interested in any negotiations that will allow me to defend my innocence.

– Agent Snow

REPORT 5. TIME STAMP:[MISSING] AGENT ID:[MISSING].

Upon further inspection of my orders for the 1903 job, I believe that I was framed by someone outside of the agency posing as a TimeWatch operative. Someone must have set me on this path to avoid being held accountable for their deeds. In an attempt to prove my innocence, I traced the source of the message to a TimeWatch HQ outpost five hours prior to my jump to 1903. I snuck past the guards, avoided any casualties, and waited for the culprit to log into the appropriate terminal.

What I saw next is hard to report without implicating myself ... or confessing to paradox effects that will surely give HQ more fodder for neutralizing me.

Unfortunately I was forced to confront my future-self logging into the terminal to send orders for the 1903 mission. I tried to stop her! She looked colder, sunken-cheeked, and emaciated. But when I confronted her and told her to surrender, she laughed at me, telling me that I "don't understand." Even though I had the upper hand physically over this clearly deranged version of myself, she seemed to know I would be there and was able to counter my every attempt to apprehend her and fled the scene before I could stop her from time jumping.

I believe that with more time I will be able to find a way to explain what happened today, but until then all I have to go on is that she told me that she no longer goes by the name Snow, but instead calls herself "Dr. Equilibrium." I can't even imagine what kind of madness would make someone (make me!) give up on my, I mean our, identity like this.

– Agent Snow

REPORT 6. TIME STAMP:[MISSING] AGENT ID:[MISSING].

I am logging this as a voluntary thought-log, as I am sure TimeWatch's Psychological Division will be asked to weigh in on my trial.

I am tired and alone, and I don't know what to believe anymore. I ran into a team of agents, and they informed me that they were not going to entertain any negotiations. Regretfully, I was forced to wound one of them in my escape. I did not wish to hurt anyone, but I'm not about to be strung up in some kangaroo court trial for crimes I didn't commit!

Since I have failed to prove my innocence again and again and without the support of TimeWatch, the paradox and time travel are almost too much to bear. I see things. I hear Dr. Equilibrium laughing at me sometimes. I look into the dark, huddled in small shacks or abandoned hallways, and I wonder what could make me into her. Or if this all a cruel joke.

I have been wondering if this could be a test of my loyalty or if I am just being naïve and should turn myself in. But just when things seem to be at their worst and I feel like giving up I find care packages. Someone knows where I am and is looking out for me. I can only hope it is someone in TimeWatch that still has faith in me and not Dr. Equilibrium playing games with my head.

In order to help myself adapt to the harsh punishment of frequent time travel I have turned to the technology produced by the shift in the timeline that I inadvertently caused: biological agents that will stabilize my DNA. I've found a few people in this timeline I can trust to keep my secret, and I've been trading engineered devices for the biochemical cocktail that keeps me sane.

Working with my hands again helps me keep my mind off of the sleep deprivation. I even feel a bit lucky when working in this timeline, because as I mentioned in my last thought-log, I often wondered what I could have created if I had stayed on Earth instead of working so hard to flee it. Folks here seem to value what I can build?

But I'm still running, and the chase is taking its toll on me physically. When I look in the mirror I can sometimes catch a glimpse of Dr. Equilibrium and the look of rage in her eyes. But that is as close as I can get to catching her.

– Agent Snow

REPORT 7. TIME STAMP:[MISSING] AGENT ID:[MISSING].

I have finally created a series of devices that can help me stabilize my own time travel without fearing that TimeWatch is tracking my movements, but they appear to be unstable. I have been wounded several times and have, several times, ended up in a different year than specified. I am still attempting to incorporate what TimeWatch technology I have access to into my own devices to counteract the variability.

I have been traveling to learn all I can about the shift and why Dr. Equilibrium may have used me to make it happen. I have studied the timeline from 1903 onward and compared it to the main timeline pre–Wright brothers shift, as well as my origin timeline, where global warming forced humanity to flee Earth in search of something more sustainable.

My findings leave me feeling conflicted. There is a balance of technology and natural environment here that I never dreamed possible. Humanity and the planet could sustain life this way indefinitely, but violence and civil unrest are everywhere. Revolutions are as frequent as forest fires, but I cannot help but feel more comfortable in this timeline than I have felt since leaving my own.

Why did this small shift produce such large results? Humanity still developed flight. People still spewed chemicals into the atmosphere. But somehow they learned to listen better to the planet. They never left for the stars. And because the planet was so small, the cities and nations and political systems couldn't contain the stress. But why would Dr. Equilibrium save a world if the people who live there will just tear it down?

– Agent Snow

REPORT 8. TIME STAMP:[MISSING] AGENT ID:[MISSING].

Still no response from any of you at TimeWatch HQ, but I don't expect one. I have had more run-ins with agents as of late and have finally been forced to look outside of TimeWatch for help (not that I ever got help from you). I have found a network of people local to this timeline that have provided me with a new, much needed, perspective on my situation, and in return I find myself swept up in their everyday troubles, trying to help where I can in this altered timeline. It feels good to be with people again. And with my knowledge of what they call "the future," I am an indispensable asset.

It is good to be wanted... It is good to be needed and I don't feel the need to prove myself to TimeWatch any longer. This reality is my reality now, and these people are my people. I will do what I can to help them carve out a future worth living.

I won't be contacting you again.

– No Longer Agent Snow

REPORT 9. TIME STAMP:[1903] AGENT ID:[MISSING].

I said I would never contact you again, but I wanted to thank you. I may have never

AGENT SNOW.

seen how perfect the 1903 mission was if you had not tried to stomp my efforts out. I also want you to know that I've won, and (you heard it here first) I will always win!

I saw myself today, a young, naïve, rough TimeWatch agent who told me to "surrender!" Call it self-fulfilling, but I couldn't help but laugh. She truly didn't understand that you had already abandoned her.

I can't believe how blind I had been! To not see how key 1903 is to building a "main timeline" that is truly worth protecting. The failure of the Wright brothers has granted me a second chance to put my engineering skills to use in creating a timeline free from the threat of global warming. Now humanity can focus on itself instead of dead-end xeno-science.

The only storm that this timeline will have to worry about is the one I will bring down upon TimeWatch if you attempt to undo the future that has been set into motion.

– Snow

REPORT 10. TIME STAMP:[MISSING] AGENT ID:[MISSING].

TimeWatch. I would like to extend my compliments to you and your agents for restoring the main timeline. Despite my best efforts to stop it, you have managed to undo everything I have worked so hard to nurture, serve, and protect. It wasn't easy to be the sole survivor of one timeline that you didn't see fit to exist, but I must be truly gifted to now be the widow of two.

I would also like to formally accept the invitation to embrace the future you so generously laid out for me. If you are wondering what that might mean for you and your agents allow me to explain. I admit guilt to all crimes committed by Dr. Equilibrium, future and past. Because when I look in the mirror I see through her eyes, I feel her rage, and I know her mission to undo future harm against Earth and humanity caused by TimeWatch is the right one.

You will hear from me again, TimeWatch, because even if you do everything in your power to undo the harms you have caused to your "main timeline," I vow to achieve balance. I will hold your agents accountable for their crimes. All of their crimes.

– Dr. Equilibrium

end

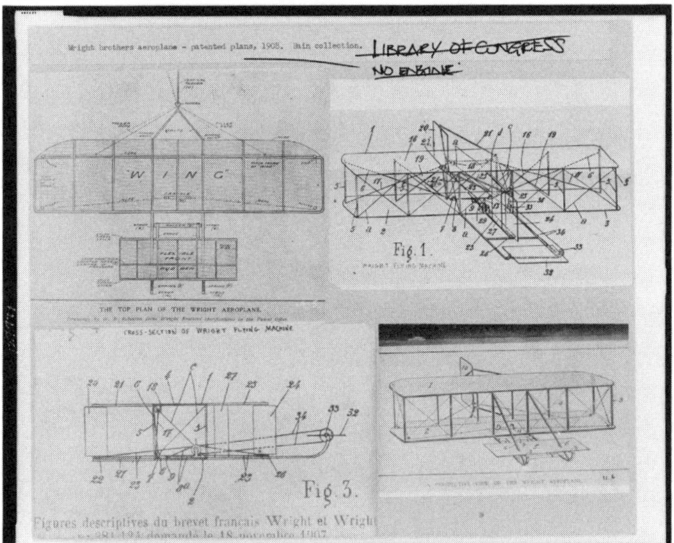
Wright brothers aeroplane - patented plans, 1908. Bain collection.
LIBRARY OF CONGRESS
NO ENGINE
W I N G
Fig. 1.
THE TOP PLAN OF THE WRIGHT AEROPLANE
CROSS-SECTION OF WRIGHT FLYING MACHINE
Fig. 3.
Figures descriptives du brevet français Wright et Wright

AGENT SNOW.

JOURNAL OF THEODOSIA BURR

THEODOSIA BURR.
1783 – 1812

THEODOSIA BURR.

3700 CE
TimeWatch HQ.

I attended Captain Yolanda Shu of the TimeWatch Unfound Book Division's patrol unit briefing this early morning. The only known copy of *De Eurois*, "About Eastern Matters," by Marcus Volcius Cerdo disappeared from the Bentley Historical Library Special Projects Collection last night. It was not stolen, though. Much worse: it was *found*.

The TimeWatch Unfound Books Division locates the lost or destroyed books in history and stores them in curated collections at the beginning of time. Like TimeWatch recruiting new blood for their organization, the Unfound Book Division rescues books from destruction right when they would otherwise burn or drown or get zapped by aliens.

Found books somehow survive their fated destruction and return to wide-availability print. These leaked books create chronal instabilities as people read them: generally small bubbles on the froth of time, but sometimes they generate these huge complex messes. Books are unpredictable beasts when they get into the hands of readers.

I always loved archaeology, and I was a classicist by previous life training. Now I hunt found books.

The Bentley Historical Library Special Projects is a closed collection accessible only by the TimeWatch Unfound Division head librarian's approval. These are history's most dangerous books. In an untainted timeline, Cerdo's *De Eurois*' existence was only known through a vague reference in Suetonius except for a few unreadable charred fragments uncovered in Herculaneum. And now Cerdo's *De Eurois* was missing from its highly defended locked glass case.

Captain Yolanda Shu informed me of a chronal instability formed in the time stream around Catholicism, Messianic Judaism, and the Reformation the same time the book disappeared from the collection shelves. The instability shoots off in so many directions it steamrolls history after the 16th century. The locus was Worms on the Rhine in 1521 – the Diet of Worms.

Someone changed the trajectory of the Reformation with a single book. My mission: remove the book from time, recover it for TimeWatch, and return it to its glass case in the Bentley Historical Library Special Projects.

THEODOSIA BURR.

1521 CE, APRIL 17
Worms, Holy Roman Empire.

Worms. This old, prosperous merchant Germany city was tense with the ongoing trial of Martin Luther at the diet. People rushed between the tall church spires through the cold German rain to their private destinations with their eyes lowered and heads bowed. Stores were closed. The taverns were crowded.

Printing was everywhere on this early morning of the Enlightenment. A local bookstore and printer sold me a copy of Luther's theses. The problem was apparent to any student of the Reformation and confirmed by my tether: instead of Luther's *95 Theses*, I held in my hands a copy of Luther's *105 Theses*. Flipping quickly through the pamphlet, I used my tether to translate the theses from their native Vulgar Latin and found references to Cerdo's *De Eurois*. Returning the bookstore, I purchased a German copy of *De Eurois* to return to TimeWatch.

I stared at the nondescript German book in my hands. This highly corrupted thing should not exist. It was a chronal anomaly bought for a single thaler.

I needed to figure out who injected this book into the time stream. By 1521, *De Eurois* was already translated from Latin into the vernacular. It had spread to the common intelligentsia. It was too late to stop the book from breaching time.
I was too far forward.

Under heavy questioning, the bookseller sent me to their master printer, Gunther Bergfalk. After a confusing conversation about the nature and philosophy of books, he found a shabby copy of Cerdo's *De Eurois* in its original Latin in the back of his shop. Gunther pointed me to the inner book plate. Original printing: Barcelona. No date.

I hopped to Barcelona to the birth of printing in Spain.

1492 CE
Barcelona, Spain.

I researched early printing in the 15th century. A tether check provided me a rough time period. Barcelona, Spain, printed its first Bible in 1473. I made an educated guess based on various other book print dates and set my autochron to Barcelona in 1492.

I stepped into the heady days of Spain at its height. The city was a riot of the old and the new. Soaring churches squatted on the once resplendent manicured lawns of Islamic mosques. Ancient Moorish fortresses were repurposed for the might of Aragon. People everywhere. *Priests* everywhere. Elsewhere, a Genoan named Columbus had just set sail for the West Indies.

In the twenty years since Barcelona built its first printing press, booksellers sprouted like weeds along the wide streets. I visited every book store. I found many copies of *The Travels of Marco Polo* and Dante's *Inferno* – the best sellers of the early days of print. And, after several days of relentless hunting, I discovered copies of Cerdo's *De Eurois* for sale in the original Latin in the small, smelly, cramped print shop of Master Printer Alonso Piero.

Master Printer Alonso accepted a commission to bind the original book four years ago from a Florentine servant eager to print his deceased master's hand-copied Latin book collection. Master Alonso had nearly passed on the commission except the text came bundled with improved copies of Virgil's popular works and a rare copy of Seneca's *Phaedra*. He printed a few copies of *De Eurois*. But, for the last several years, *De Eurois* had sold briskly, so he kept it in print. From fulfilled orders, he guessed copies had spread to Venice, Florence, Bruges, Magdeburg, and ... maybe Toledo.

I asked Master Alonso for the name of the Florentine servant's master. After several hours of searching through ancient, dusty account books, he found it: *Bracciolini*. Print date: 1476.

I asked to see the original manuscript. The master found it in a locked, disused cabinet under discarded printing-press parts and thrust it in my face. But this copy of the book was a handwritten copy of an original. Where was the original?

In the accounts next to the date and title was the name of the servant: Mafeo Buscharino of Florence. Florence was my next stop ... further back in time.

1476 CE
Republic of Florence.

I made a short time hop to Florence across a fifteen years gulf.

I tracked down the name *Bracciolini* to the family of the deceased Gian Francesco Poggio Bracciolini, secretary to seven popes and infamous book hunter and collector – better known as Poggio Florentinus or Poggio the Florentine. Throughout his life, he kept a circle of fellow book-loving New Humanist friends and died a wealthy man in 1459.

Poggio Florentinus' few remaining Florentine living relatives and old friends remembered a household servant named Mafeo Buscharino. He was a large, serious man with imposing eyebrows and heavy jaw. He worked in the employ of the family for a brief time. But no one paid him to carry Cerdo's *De Eurois* to Barcelona for printing. Barcelona? Those filthy Spanish? Master Poggio's books belong in Florence!

No, their grandfather left nothing in a will about having his books distributed after his death. Poggio Florentinus lacked any interest in sharing his books outside his circle during his lifetime; he was only interested in translating and reading them with his friends. Most of his books were still where he left them when he died – moldering away in his closed, tiny study upstairs in the family Florentine townhouse.

Other time travelers were afoot. I guessed Mafeo Buscharino stole the manuscript from Poggio Florentinus' locked collection. He had the book printed in Spain when it was in danger of being again consumed by time but left a purposeful trail of authenticity to fuse the book to the time stream for any later nosey book archaeologists.

It was impossible to calculate the precise date when the book was stolen. It happened some rough time between Poggio's death and 1476. Hunting Mafeo between the two dates to a precise time when he was both employed by the family and before he stole the book meant possibly dozens of random time jumps – and those jumps would not allow me to remove the book cleanly anyway. It had touched too many minds and souls.

I was robbed of a simpler time jump to conclude my mission. I was still on the hunt for *De Eurois*' genesis.

I took an opportunity to pass an afternoon with Caterina Brexiano, an aging daughter of another old Florentine book hunter and fellow New Humanist with deep connections to Poggio. Knowing the corrupted timeline German translation was in my pack, I probed her knowledge of *De Eurois*. Did Caterina's father ever borrow the book from Poggio?

Yes, they traded the book back and forth for a while, and, long ago, she had read it. Cerdo's *De Eurois* glorified the Roman Empire and Far Eastern rule under their client king, Herod Antipas, Caterina said. Most of the book focused on Rome's struggles with the Parthian Empire and the lives of the Roman governors. Roughly it covered the political history of Iudaea from 6 CE until the financial crisis under Caligula in approximately 40 CE.

In Caterina's opinion, the book was just another Roman history like Tacitus or Suetonius. But . . . a look of consternation came over her face. There were . . . things . . . mentions . . .

When did Poggio Florentinus find Cerdo's *De Eurois*, I asked? When he started on his mad book-collecting enterprise, Caterina said: the Convocation of Constance between 1414 and 1418.

1417 CE
Convocation of Constance, Holy Roman Empire.

I found young Poggio Florentinus in a tavern in Constance in 1417 drinking tankards of heavy brown beer. He complained bitterly about Hungarian religious reformer Jan Hus' condemnation and execution by burning at the hands of the Church. An unfair judgment! Hus was simply a man pointing out the foibles of the Church, a Church built on foibles! And nothing was going well for his employer, the pope, either. The pope wasn't coming out of this whole pope-antipope argument as the actual pope. Not that Pope John XXIII was anything more than a sleazy pirate in the pockets of the Medici, that corrupt bastard.

Gian Francesco Poggio Bracciolini, young secretary to the pope in service to the Curia was going be dealing with a whole new pope and pope entourage soon. Poggio was bored. He had done nothing for years except sit in taverns in this dull town on the Rheine and argue with duller priests. What was the educated man to do?

But, Poggio had a fun idea to alleviate his boredom. He heard the Benedictine monastery of St. Gertrude up in the Alps had an untouched and extensive library. He was arranging an expedition. Legend had it, Petrarch pieced together Livy's long-lost *The History of Rome* from forgotten manuscripts found in libraries in Alpine monasteries. Maybe Poggio will have similar luck with St. Gertrude. They leave in two days. Did I want in?

I queried my tether about the Benedictine monastery of St. Gertrude as I prepared to join Poggio Florintinus' expedition. I roughly planned to break into the library, steal the book from the timeline, and correct the chronal instability by heist. This, I thought, was the origin of *De Eurois* in time.

Then I learned surprising news: in the correct timeline, the Benedictine monastery of St. Gertrude ceased to exist by fire in 1292.

The book, the monastery, and this expedition were all part of the same corrupted timeline. According to my tether, in 1417, Poggio Florentinus raided a different Alpine monastery (how many were there? "Lots," said my tether) to discover a much different book. And I learned which book it was: Lucretius' *De Rerum Natura*. My time traveling book thieves had exchanged one dangerous ancient Roman book for another.

Someone was covering their tracks with double blinds. Someone knew TimeWatch would send a patrol unit after them.

I had to get to that monastery, *De Eurois* in 1292, and ensure the monastery burnt down so Poggio the Florentine would steal the correct book and prod along the Enlightenment without destroying the Reformation first.

1292 CE, JANUARY 11
St. Gertrude Monastery, Nyons.

In the summer of 1291, Pope Nicholas IV, vicar of Rome, ordered a convocation of the Benedictine and Dominican monks and nuns to gather at St. Gertrude Monastery outside of Nyons and argue the greatest theological question of their time. Here, in this refrigerator of a building complex high in the Alps, they debated the core tenant of transubstantiation. How can Jesus' body, which stands at the right hand of the Father, also be physically present in the Eucharist at Mass? How can he be at both places at once?

The debate had stalemated.

It was January 11th by the not-yet-invented Gregorian calendar and, freezing and in hip deep snowfall, I climbed the mountain to the monastery with the other last straggling brothers and sisters joining the convocation. After we crossed the gate, greeted the other brothers and sisters, and had some hot stew, I broke off from the group and wandered the grounds.

Connected to the main cloister were the church, the refectory, the infirmary, the stables, the balneary, the scriptorium, and the library. The library itself was a tall octagonal building with few windows connected to the scriptorium by a covered stone hallway. It was blocked from the inside by a heavy wood and iron door, and had no external access and few high, slit windows too small for a person to climb through. The building, a small but solid work of early Dark Ages architecture, was designed by frightened people to keep the Vandals, Visigoths, Ostrogoths, and other invading barbarians from destroying their books.

My scanner picked up thousands of highly flammable books inside.

The librarian, Brother Heinrich of Wetzlar, had the only key to the heavy oak and iron door barricading the library. Standing in the scriptorium while monks bent at desks winced in the dying midwinter light scratching out the Books of the Bible on vellum with stubs of charcoal, the librarian informed me no one enters the library except himself. He, and he alone, decides who sees which books. The books were between him and God.

Librarians are all the same.

1292 CE, JANUARY 15
St. Gertrude Monastery, Nyons.

A few days later, on the 15th, I snuck out of the convocation in my impersonator mesh and used my tether to scan a detailed map of the library from the outside. I also met various monks and nuns of the order. I especially enjoyed the company of the old blind library brother Mathis of Willa.

I asked Brother Mathis about Cerdo's *De Eurois*. He remembered it. A centuries-old book and not particularly religious. Part of the original collection, he said, from before the cloister was a monastery and when it was a military fortress. It sat on the south side of the library with the rest of the original collection. Cold kept the bugs away. Bring that book to the convocation, he said to me. It would solve their conundrum!

I was also lightly menaced by the imposing dark-browed Dominican friar, Brother Otto of Rottweil. Sometimes the portly monk Brother Eberhard of Freiberg followed me through the halls at a discrete distance. Both were from the same monastery, foreign to St. Gertrude.

1292 CE, JANUARY 17
St. Gertrude Monastery, Nyons.

And two days later in the dining hall Brother Eberhard jumped me.

We struggled. We knocked over hot bowls of stew.

The portly brother clung to my back. I elbowed him in the ribs, grabbed a wooden spoon and smacked him. In return, he punched me hard in the kidneys.

I bowed over, gasping for breath.

Thinking I was done, Eberhard pulled a jagged-edged knife from his belt. I dodged his thrust, shoved him against a table, and managed a lucky grip on a handful of cassock. He thrashed and swore in a surprising mash of English and Chinese. I jammed the PaciFist neural disruptor into his neck and stabbed the button.

Brother Eberhard collapsed with a thud.

I searched him quickly and pulled back in shock when his disheveled cassock fell away from a black tattoo on his chest. A symbol I recognized: the Discontinuity.

I knew these guys.

The Discontinuity smashes the edifices of control by manipulating history

THEODOSIA BURR.

and erasing rich and powerful human organizations from existence. These violent anarchists mold time around their twisted political ideals of freedom. They want bigger fiery explosions and more war and constant mayhem and death to history's privileged. Destroy all the corporations. Erase all the religions. Behead all the government officials. Set the small, the weak, and the disempowered free!

Last time I fought the Discontinuity was in the midst of a beam weapon battle during the storming of the Bastille.

The Reformation. The hundred years of even more brutal war. The crippling of religious institutions and the rise of a different sort of messianic mania. With a single, simple, lost book. Make time bow to the lost writing of one long dead man. I searched Eberhard's pockets. At first, nothing – a rosary, some charcoal, a dried leaf. Then I found a slowing decaying folded piece of lined paper written in ball-point pen. Not a thing of the late 13th century. It said

3/5/455 – Noviodunum – K Tranquillus – Time Watch – Plan B

I wanted more detailed information about the Discontinuity before I stopped this "Plan B." When was their first forward-time public appearance? My tether advised New York and the 24th century.

2348 CE
Neo New York.

Graffitied mile-high sluice gates protected Manhattan's canals from the angry encroaching ocean. The thrum of skyscraper-like pumps was the background music to 24th-century New York life. Technology preserved the island, its millions of inhabitants, and its financial empire against nature and a too-warm Earth.

I took the hover train downtown to Wall St. A man with a head clothed in neurochips pushed past me in a hurry. Two women, disembarking side by side, gabbed loudly to the air and not to each other. Bright advertisements on walls in a mash of English and Chinese read my DNA and flashed me an algorithmically enticing product. A panhandler begged for cash to buy holo time. The sidewalks were sidewalks.

Things were going down. Emergency crews rushed past me toward the New York Fed building. Drones screamed by overhead to record the exciting event and then, inexplicably, stopped in midair to project enormous Jumbotron-sized screens on building sides for the gawkers. Neo-bankers stopped yelling into the air as one to turn and stare into space at their inter-cranial Internet feeds. Sirens wailed far off down the street.

The ancient downtown building was on fire: a controlled enormous smiley-face burn with a projected holographic Discontinuity symbol as the nose.

The air crackled with a puff of ozone as hidden old-technology speakers leapt to life. The drone-projected holos jiggered, wavered, and suddenly, staring down at me across space and time 50 feet tall in full triple surround sound was the heavy browed, steely glare of Discontinuity's leader, Dominican brother Otto of Rottwiel. No, not Otto. Nor the Florentine Mafeo Buscharino. Discontinuity's leader, Maximillian Saladin.

Next to him, shadowy, was the future-time version of portly Brother Eberhard. Maximillian Saladin gave his one-day-to-be-famous speech about freedom and hegemony and blowing it all to smithereens. The rallying call of a brand new Vladimir Lenin or Mao Tse-tung. The dawn of a new age free of all this technology and messy banking.

While Saladin growled his twisted philosophy and police hackers tried to shut him down, I pushed through the enraptured crowd – New Yorkers of any time period will stop for a spectacle – and stepped into an alley. Needing to stop the Discontinuity, I programmed my autochron with one remaining lead. The dates on Brother Eberhard's decaying yellow lined paper: March 5th, 455 CE.

455 CE, MARCH 5
Noviodunum, Western Roman Empire.

Funny thing about the smell of charred human bodies: they smell like pork.

Noviodunum, whatever it once was to the Western Roman Empire, was an ex-city in March of 455 CE. It had the rough outlines of a city and some puritanically straight Roman roads, but the Vandals had crushed the essential city-ness from it. I spotted one last standing building: a white stucco-walled villa in the midst of perfectly manicured and empty farm plots up the hill and protected by stands of trees. I could see perfect inlaid mosaics on the floor through the open front door. In the courtyard a mule, hitched to a small cart filled with chairs and boxes, brayed.

A tired old man in a dirty white toga and grey hair cut in the Roman fashion emerged from the house with arms laden with heavy codices. He dumped them unceremoniously into the cart with a thud. Then, seeing me for the first time, he made shooing motions at me. Go away. It's not safe.

I assured him in tether-translated perfect Empire Latin I was not with the barbarians sacking the town.

He said nothing was left but enemies in this world.

He introduced himself as Kaeso Aquillius Tranquillus. His family lived in this villa for generations. These farms were his farms; the villagers his villagers. Now his family was dead. His villagers were dead. The town of Noviodunum was dead. He was the last and he was taking his possessions into the mountains where the Roman legions hid. This was the End Times.

Kaeso charged back inside to gather another armload of possessions. While he was away, I leaned into his cart and searched the codices. I picked up one bound in grey leather and flipped through it. I squinted. I clicked on my tether to translate the text and began to skim. These books have neither title nor index pages, but I felt certain I was holding that one copy of *De Eurois*. I hurriedly put it back. No removing the book from the timeline ... yet. Too early.

Just as Kaeso emerged from his doorway, the ground shook with the pounding of hooves. We watched a single armed leather-and-iron-clad rider thunder up that perfect Roman road. I fingered the PaciFist in my pocket, but I'm not a particularly good shot, and hitting a rider on horseback would be tricky at best.

Kaeso reached into his wagon, pushed away some old shoes, and pulled out an iron gladius. He held it limply in one hand.

The rider pulled off his helmet. Eberhard of Freiberg. Or, in this timeline, Eberhard the Vandal. The necklace of human teeth was a nice touch – although not necessarily culturally appropriate.

"Oh, TimeWatch, I'm not his enemy," Eberhard leered in his mixture of English and Chinese as he reined in his horse. "I'm here to make sure the old man lives to reach the fortress. With, you know, the book."

We were silent.

Eberhard gestured toward the mountains with a tip of a badly made iron sword. "I'm the bodyguard. The insurance policy. Glad to see you took my simple bait. You're going to die out here, TimeWatch. A nice time and place for it. Twenty-five-hundred years from now, you will be just another archaeological dig."

"Murderer!" Kaeso Aquillius Tranquillus hissed, mistaking the 24th-century speech for East Germanic. "You and your kind murdered my wife! My son!"

Eberhard look vaguely annoyed and took a swipe at me with his iron sword, but he was from a far-off future and had no training in Dark Ages weaponry. I jumped back, and the swipe went wide. Eberhard laughed merrily. Missing didn't bother him.

He guided his horse around for another pass, this time getting lucky and nicking me in the shoulder.

The pain shot through my arm.

Eberhard flipped the sword around in the air like a showman and then thrust the business end down at my face.

I flipped on the PaciFist and, instead of going for Eberhard, I zapped the horse in the neck. The PaciFist couldn't take down a horse, but it certainly startled it. The horse reared in fright and threw Eberhard violently to the ground. No stirrups.

As Eberhard struggled to get up and push his helmet out of his eyes, Kaeso Aquillius Tranquillus stabbed him once in the shoulder, knocking him back down. Eberhard hissed.

The second time, Kaeso, once a young legionnaire, pulled his weapon out of Eberhard's shoulder and stabbed the Discontinuity agent in the throat. Eberhard fell.

"It fails to burn!" Eberhard the Vandal gurgled at me as the hole in his neck spewed blood. "We rescued the library right after you left! This changes nothing!"

He laughed. He coughed. And on the ground, he died.

We stared at the body of the pseudo-Vandal. Was leaving Eberhard here a mistake in time? Did it matter? One dead Vandal among thousands in this time and place in the destroyed towns of the dying Western Empire. What did he say? To be part of an archaeological dig?

We left the body for the crows.

Kaeso bound the wound on my shoulder. An hour later, he started to drive his possessions, his cart, and his mule up the mountain to the safety of the old Roman fortress which became St. Gertrude Monastery.

With Kaeso gone, I healed myself and triggered my autochron. I returned to the monastery and the fire.

1292 CE, FEBRUARY 9
St. Gertrude Monastery.

I headed again to the library to deal with the librarian, Brother Heinrich of Wetzlar, except Brother Heinrich was unconscious on the floor. The monks had fled the scriptorium. The key was gone. The ancient wood and iron library door hung open. I slid through a dark stone tunnel to emerge into a dimly lit room. The library was almost pitch black except for slivers of light from high narrow windows and the rare candle stub. The religious books slumped in an untidy pile by the entrance. Others were crammed on shelves and heaped to the ceiling on tables and covered in dust.

I heard two echoing voices arguing: Abbot Werner and Brother Otto of Rottweil ne' Maximillian Saladin. Abbot Werner was adamant. And drunk. This pagan knowledge within these library walls tainted the holy debate about God and transubstantiation. The convocation failed. He was made a fool before the blessed pope. Fault sat with this building of ancient lies. Burn the books!

I couldn't hear what Brother Otto said in reply as the stacks muffled his voice. It sounded gentle, soothing, and fatherly. See, burning the library down was a poor life choice.

Brother Mathis had said earlier *De Eurois* was in the southern part of the library. I powered my impersonator mesh and slipped on my night vision glasses. The library sprung into sharp relief in hues of greens and blacks.

I carefully climbed over books to reach the library's southernmost point. These ancient books had no identifying names, and the monks piled them randomly in jumbled heaps. I looked for a grey leather-bound book in this area . . . it was difficult to make out colors with the night vision glasses so I pushed them back on my head.

There. Under the pile on my left. I dug through the books. I lifted the dust-covered codex and opened it. I pulled the German version of the book from my pack. My tether informed me I found a high probability textual match. The mission parameters stated the TimeWatch Unfound Book Division librarian wanted her book back in its glass case. It can't burn and it can't stay here. It must come home with me.

As I slid the book into my pack, I heard breathing and the crunch of papers under a foot. I turned. Brother Otto of Rottweil, wearing his own night vision glasses, stood in the arch between the south annex and library center.

I let out a tiny gasp.

Otto lifted a palm-sized beam weapon and fired.

I dived. The beam barely missed my head and hit a bookcase. A book sizzled. A flame popped. Was this the start of the fire?

He cursed loudly and fired his gun again.

I fled through the stacks with *De Eurois*. I heard Otto in pursuit. I shoved books off a table into his path and leapt over a table. I ran for the blip of light marking the hallway between the library and the scriptorium.

My nose filled with the smell of old, dry paper meeting flame.

I heard a series of thuds. I rounded a corner in time to watch Abbot Werner knock over a stack and pass out drunk on the floor. What to do. What to do! Does the Abbot die here? I don't know: history doesn't record that detail. The library is burning. And Abbot Werner isn't thin.

Damn my humanity. I struggled with Abbot Werner's heavy body while I heard Brother Otto roar in anger at the black sooty smoke in the air. Why do these monks weigh so much? Where did they get all the food? Even with structural help from my TimeWatch uniform I was heaving. My eyes burned. Just a few more feet...

I dropped the abbot in the hall between the scriptorium and the library. Fresh air. I heard voices of yelling monks. Get water from the horse trough. The library is burning!

I had only a minute before the scriptorium was swarming with monks and nuns. I stopped and retched up some black tarry substance out of my lungs. Oily smoke billowed through the open door. I could hear Otto roar inside – in anger, not in pain.

Hiding behind a copyists' platform, I unfolded the autochron and held both ends tightly. With *De Eurois* safely in my pack, the library on fire, and the book removed from time, I returned to report to TimeWatch.

Look, Captain Yolanda Shu! Another fine success!

end

ST. GERTRUDE MONASTERY, NYON.

THEODOSIA BURR.

JOURNAL OF THE SURGEON, AND OTHERS.

AMELIA EARHART.
1897 –

TEMPLETON GRAVES.
1926 –

THE SURGEON AND OTHERS.

12584 BCE, AUGUST: TEMPLETON GRAVES.

The paradox is manageable, but extensive. I did the best I could to wipe out all evidence of their prehistoric high-tech "golden age" to say nothing of the islands themselves, but there's little bits of evidence all over. Quite frankly I'm not sure the fabric of space-time is ever going to fully recover, especially in the swath of empty sea southwest of Bermuda where the capital was. Unfortunate, but honestly it's the best you're going to get when you ask for a job like this.

I've got the ringleader – Atlas – stashed in chrono-stasis in low Earth orbit. You can find the physical and chronological coordinates at the standard drop site under the Sphinx. Just off the Nile Delta. Funny thing: a whole civilization subsumed but the rubbish cat statue sticks around.

The erosion patterns are going to confuse them terribly, but you just sprinkle a few records around the Egyptian Old Kingdom and eventually even the pharaohs will think they put it there. Make a note that someone should do that.

Fair warning, you're also going to find a lot of stone circles. Like, a lot. I'm not sure what it is, but I think the geomagnetic alignments make them tachyon resistant.

The crystals, even the big ones, are all inaccessible – sunk, along with the whole bloody continent – thanks to some extensive tectonic re-engineering. You're welcome.

I checked: Plato's histories are now just philosophical treatises, but they still talk about the place, which should give us cover for any other surviving records.

In short: Atlantis is gone.

I am sure an unending shower of praise awaits me at the Citadel. Maybe a parade.

1958 CE, NOVEMBER 16: AMELIA EARHART.

Begin tether recording.

REDACTED: This is strictly off the books? No records?

Earhart: [sigh] Would I come to you if it was any other way?

REDACTED: So you're not recording this?

THE SURGEON AND OTHERS.

Earhart: Of course not!

REDACTED: A little enthusiastic, there. You sure? [threatening] No records. Not now, not ever. Not if you want my help. [playfully] Regardless, you understand, you get caught and this is the kind of thing that ends up with you on a forced retirement in some pocket universe on the other side of never. Peaceful, sure, but the neural reconstruction they give you after the MEM-tag is going to leave you just this side of lobotomized. If you get caught.

Earhart: [nervously] I ... I understand. [muffled] Just coffee for me, thanks.

REDACTED: You understand how my fee works? I got your down payment, or I wouldn't be here. But you get it, right? I don't negotiate. [muffled] Honey, I'll take a coffee and a piece of that apple pie if you don't mind.

Earhart: You do this for us, you can set your price.

REDACTED: [laughing] I always do. So what's the job?

Earhart: Earlier this morning, the Pentagon discovered the designs for an honest-to-God death ray. Part of the DARPA program Ike just started to try to catch up with the Soviets after Sputnik. Within three years the program will be in full swing at Martin Marietta in Denver, and ...

REDACTED: [interrupting] Sounds pretty standard. Let me guess? Don't let this anachronistic technology upset the careful balance of blah blah blah ... ? Some future super-patriot decides to help knock the Communists out of the Cold War before the Russians could do it to themselves?

Earhart: No ... it's ... it's a little more complicated than that. It's Atlantean.

[pause]

REDACTED: Bullshit. Atlantis is a myth. A never-was.

Earhart: Well, it is now, and that's the way it ought to be. But it ... uh ... well, we might have had a hand in making it a myth.

THE SURGEON AND OTHERS.

REDACTED: Not enough of one, apparently. Who's the screwup?

[pause]

Earhart: I'd rather not say.

REDACTED: Then no deal. I gotta know who I'm working around, or this has no chance of success.

Earhart: Fine. [deep breath] It was [inaudible].

REDACTED: Who?

Earhart: [louder] Graves.

REDACTED: [agitated, almost shouting] *Graves*!? [hushed] Graves! No wonder you're having problems! Graves is a butcher! And an idiot! He's got no finesse! I mean that son of a bi–

Earhart: He's already been . . retired. This is no longer about him. This is about you. Can you clean up the mess he made? Stop the recursion – quietly – so that no one else needs to be retired?

REDACTED: I want 1,400,000 late 20th-century Jordanian dinar in nonsequential small bills, Vermeer's original *Girl With a Pearl Earring*, and a 1968 Dodge Charger. In orange. Fresh off the assembly line, please. Plus expenses. I'll leave the temporal-spatial coordinates for the drop site under this napkin. I walk out of here, and you don't see me until the job is done. Got it?

Earhart: Got it.

REDACTED: [muffled] Sorry about the pie, ma'am. My friend here will eat it. And pick up the tab. Thank you kindly.

[long pause]

Earhart: [whispered] He's in.

THE SURGEON AND OTHERS.

End tether recording.

1958 CE, NOVEMBER 17: THE SURGEON

The problem is that somebody always remembers. You do whatever you can to minimize the paradox, sure, but little bits of it just get stuck.

Sometimes it's stuff, little things the rewritten universe just forgot to rewrite: an iron hammer left over in a 75-million-year-old limestone concretion, or a picture of a helicopter carved into the wall of an Egyptian temple.

Sometimes it's places, a few squares miles here or there where that closed-off alternate timeline peeks through no matter how many times you try to patch over it, like that little slice of the neo-Triassic that keeps bleeding over into that lake in Scotland.

More often it's people. People not quite drawn all the way into that tachyon tidal wave when the timeline rights itself. Oracles, prophets, and – yeah – madmen. But consciously or not they can see the imperfections left from your handiwork, like when you look at a wall that's been painted, repainted, and then repainted again. More often than not it's just a little sense of déjà vu, not too different than that fuzzy-headed feeling you get after being MEM-tagged. But sometimes it's bigger. Somebody who remembers all the inventions you couldn't let Tesla keep, or – better example – all those folks who freaked out when they heard *The War of the Worlds* because at some deep, subconscious level they remembered it happening.

When the things they remember are . . . troublesome, that's when I get involved.

If you want to be coarse about it, I'm a cleaner.

But I prefer to think of myself as a surgeon.

«later»

The trick about living freelance in this business is that you don't always have all the tools that the big boys have. Well, big girls if you count Amelia. You work for TimeWatch, and you can throw questions at an eternal quantum supercomputer that contains the sum of all sentient knowledge all day long.

Me? I got a copy of the 1913 *Encyclopedia Britannica* for research, and if I can't find what I need there, I hoof it to the library.

But it keeps the mind agile, not having a tether to depend on. You get a little used to thinking sideways about problems like this. Turns out Graves did a good-enough job that official records weren't going to get me far in tracking down when and where Atlantean recursions are going to happen. But somebody does know.

Somebody always remembers.

1887 CE, MARCH 18: THE SURGEON

It's Edgar Cayce's tenth birthday, today. And today, he started hearing voices. He can't understand most of what they're saying, and he's convinced that at least one of them is his maternal grandmother. He thinks the rest are angels. At least he hopes they're angels, because he's a good kid. That's what his diary says, anyway. Terrible handwriting.

He goes on to be one of the most famous mediums of the 20th century. A prophet of sorts. One of the most common themes of his readings?

Atlantis.

My best guess is that the kid's brain is catching delta-wave interference from some closed-off alternate timeline where Graves never quite knocked Atlantis off the map. Just bum luck and atypical neural oscillation, apparently. I won't be able to tell for sure until I can take an EEG, but I don't want to spook the kid or his parents. Not until he can point me in the right direction.

«later»

Snuck into the house again to run the EEG. Had to gas the place to keep everyone asleep but Edgar, and even then had to leave the kid with some pretty extensive posthypnotic suggestion to keep him from remembering what I did. Thank God none of the neighbors saw.

The readings are off the charts. Whatever this kid is getting, he's getting a lot of it, all the time. Earhart seemed to hint that the recursion was just beginning in 1958, but I wouldn't be surprised if Graves' sloppy work hadn't let something back in sooner.

If it was ever really gone at all.

I put a subdermal transmitter behind his ear while the kid was out, set to start recording in about 1905 when his readings and predictions start to hit the papers. Shouldn't interfere with whatever vibrations he's picking up, but I need to know what the kid is saying.

THE SURGEON AND OTHERS.

1933 CE, JULY 6: THE SURGEON

Edgar is famous by now: a professional medium with a staff of employees and volunteers. But still, he's got followers. Hell – they built him a school and a hospital at Virginia Beach, where the "sand crystals" can resonate with the "healing energies" coming from inside the planet.

It took my ... uh ... borrowed equipment a few hours to transcribe and cross-reference the recordings from the subdermal transmitter, but I've got a good body of information to go by. More than I could pull together from the library, anyway.

He's just hearing one voice now, and only when he's sleeping or in a trance. Sounds like things went quiet for a while until he met a hypnotist in 1901. That's ... new. Probably my fault.

He calls it "the entity," but it knows too much about what's happening now, in this universe, to be tuning in from outside. Whatever he's talking to – whatever's talking through him – is still here.

He's getting a lot about Atlantis. Lots of extraneous detail that isn't going to help me much: lots about energy-transmitting crystals, magnetic fields, and elevated souls. He keeps coming back to some giant crystal at the center of the old city – calls it the "Tuaoi Stone" or the "Great Crystal" – that harnessed all sorts of ambient energy to power their civilization. Sounds a little bit like the scalar resonant transduction interferometers that power TimeWatch's autochrons.

Just yesterday he mentioned the "death-ray" from '58. Said it'd be rediscovered within 25 years, and that it would be based on that same Atlantean crystal technology. Point to Amelia for honesty, point to Cayce for accuracy. But how did they build it? Cayce's not giving anybody enough details to be able to put any of that to use.

«later»

Another lead. Way back in March 1932, "the entity" declares that part of the old kingdom will be rediscovered near Bimini in 1968, or maybe 1969, at the crest of a sunken mountain from the lost continent. The beginning of the "rising of Atlantis."

Cayce's version of events is geologically improbable to say the least, but depending on how much alteration Graves made to the tectonic subsidence patterns before he got his gold pocket watch and a one-way ticket out of the time stream, he might not be entirely wrong.

«later»

The prophecies are starting to take a dark turn. Earthquakes. Floods. Pole shifts. Climatic upheaval. California sliding into the Pacific. New York washed away in a tidal wave, most of the Carolinas, Georgia, and a good share of Europe lost to incessant flooding. The death ray is bad... the rest? The rest could be worse.

No wonder TimeWatch reached out.

Whatever Graves did was not enough. This time stream – my time stream – is like a rubber band twisted, twisted, and twisted again. As long as you're holding on to the ends it holds its shape, but you let go? It snaps back, quick, and all the quicker if you have it wound tight.

Is Bimini where the rubber band starts to snap back into its old shape?

Or did Graves wind it so tight that it's starting to break?

1968 CE, SEPTEMBER 2: THE SURGEON

I keep my distance while Valentine and his friends investigate the stones. They really do look like a road. I traced the first historical reference to them back to this date – not sure yet if Valentine really discovered them, or if they just weren't here yesterday. Getting accurate readings is going to be a big problem if this is part of the recursion – one day there's nothing, and then the next there's a big tachyon fluctuation and bam! Now there's something there that, for all the universe is concerned, has always been there.

I couldn't jump directly here. Buzzed Lakeland, Florida, on the way in. Nothing that should interfere with the contract, but not my usual precision. Not sure if it's another remnant of Graves' sloppy work, or if there's something else interfering with my equipment.

I've got an updated set of Cayce's readings to go through. Seems like Bimini came up a few more times in readings before he died in 1945, primarily as the last resting place of an Atlantean hall of records designed to survive the cataclysm that would wipe their civilization out. Did they, I wonder, see TimeWatch coming?

«later»

I've got core samples from the Bimini road for additional analysis back at the lab. Once Valentine surfaced, I de-cloaked and cruised toward the other anomaly, a few miles toward Andros. The one they call the Temple. It looks a little like a Mayan stepped pyramid, but not so close that you couldn't convince yourself it was a natural phenomenon. I see evidence of drilling not too far distant, not fresh. Probably 20 years old. Maybe somebody beat Valentine out here?

Once I get close, my instruments go crazy. I can't jump out – probably for the same reason I couldn't jump in. There's definitely something down here. Something big, interfering with quantum teleportation in a major way.

Oh... oh no. Diverting power to engines now! It's... [static]

2024 CE, AUGUST 3: THE SURGEON

The recursion is in full swing, now. I shouldn't stay here long. Once I got clear of its interference I jumped forward, but there's no way I'm going to be able to regroup here.

No. Wait. I need to get this down.

I had to sacrifice the submersible to get away from the thing at Bimini: a giant crystal in some kind of half-engineered magma chamber surrounded by standing stones. I can't be certain without a lot more data, but I have a good feeling that it was the "entity" influencing Cayce, and maybe also the thing he was calling the Hall of Records.

The geomagnetic stress the planet is under by now is extensive, but it's only a symptom of the underlying stress the quantum-mechanical foundations of this whole sector of the galaxy are under. Refugees from both coasts are surging toward the American heartland, but communications between East and West are down: Atlantean colonies all along the Mississippi Valley are interfering with microwave and satellite transmission even where they're not in open war with the locals: death ray versus death ray. Silver lining: at least now we know who (and what) the Mound Builders were.

It didn't take long to draw attention to myself when I got here. Seems like these Atlanteans are highly familiar with time travel technology: I had a whole squad on me within a few minutes of arrival, probably tracking my Tempus, but I managed to win free with the help of a Centauri particle disruptor I keep for emergencies. I didn't have to use it, but just pointing it at them seemed to have the desired effect.

My translator is on the fritz, but it was clear what they were looking for: TimeWatch agents. Never have I been so glad that I don't have an autochron or a tether.

Completely deniable.

Probably why TimeWatch hired me.

TIMEWATCH HQ: AMELIA EARHART

Agent, this data file is damaged. Access denied. Please try a different query.

Clearance Epsilon Seven acknowledged. Insufficient clearance. Access denied. Please try a different query.

Clearance override Omega Twelve acknowledged. Accessing data file. Agent, this data file is damaged but partially recoverable. Begin playback?

Graves has been ... dealt with. [static] ... on is on board. He knows nothing. But I remain confident that he has the best chance of containing any rebel efforts to ... [long burst of static] ... minimum of additional chronal disturbance. I am concerned, howev ... [long burst of static] ... our role in the original colony ... [static] ... resulting conflict. I continue to monitor his progress, and will ensure that there are no loose ends once this is done.

[long burst of static]

File ends.

Agent, do you have another query?

Accessing data files relating to Agent Templeton Graves. 129 data files recovered. Begin playback?"

14 BCE, JUNE 11: THE SURGEON

It's amazing how quick it all comes back to you, going back to the belly of the beast. Brought a few Atlantean foot soldiers with me to ... distract ... everyone still in the TimeWatch safe house while I accessed their computer and hacked into Earhart's personnel file. Anyone not dealing directly with the incursion was searching for the chronal breach, so it was damn near deserted, and me? Well, I had the central computer station all to myself.

Almost everything related to me was either triple encrypted or simply deleted. Had to call in a favor to find someone with a high enough clearance to recover whatever was left of the data file. In a business like mine, sometimes all you've got is favors. Thank you, Ronald Reagan. I hope when they find out you helped me the reconstructed memories they give you before dumping you back out into the time stream are good ones. Something Hollywood, maybe. Hell – they should make you president.

I had a little help on the inside, sure, but someone else is helping Amelia cover her tracks, and Graves, for all his idiocy, is probably dead. This really is off the books.

I'm not going to let the local space-time system collapse, and I'm not going to let some fugitive civilization re-rewrite 15,000 years of established history. I'm a fan of Earth. My parents are from here.

But I still don't like getting played.

Between my own research and his mission files, I think I have a good idea of where to start on putting everything back in its place, and preventing this recursion from ever occurring.

«later»

All it takes is a little alcohol and some good-natured fear-mongering, and yeah – you can get the better part of a Roman legion fired up enough to start pushing over standing stones on the middle of Salisbury Plain. Just spread around a little story about druids and child sacrifice, and man, those guys will just go. to. town.

The stone circles aren't just a quirk of Graves' sloppy work. They're part of a leave-behind system anticipating TimeWatch's attempt to root them out. Those geomagnetic alignments bled off just enough ambient energy that the last few seed crystals could regrow their memory matrices without TimeWatch noticing. Pretty smart, actually.

Of course, you knock a few – or basically all – of those stone circles out of alignment, and the crystals don't grow as well, or as quickly. That geomagnetic transduction field doesn't work as well, and the whole system starts to overload with chronometric feedback.

It should give me some time to deal with the recursion before it gets into full swing, but as a side effect some of the sites snapped out of the system at different times than others.

They were all poorly understood, so the paradox has been minor, but I have to say I'm a little amused that if you dig now it looks like all these sites are different ages. Good luck, archaeologists. And sorry.

1901 CE, APRIL 21: THE SURGEON

Had to make sure my little game with the stone circles hadn't killed the goose that laid the golden egg. I wouldn't have been able to make any of these connections without Cayce, so I doubled back to catch him while he was still in Kentucky.

THE SURGEON AND OTHERS.

He's still in contact with the Tuaoi Stone: probably the same crystal I saw off of Andros. Good. Without his readings, I'd be dealing with some pretty serious paradox, maybe be in danger of getting subsumed myself. Glad my calculations were correct.

I can tell, though, that I've had some effect. Edgar lost his voice for an entire year, and only just got it back last night with the help of a traveling hypnotist: Harry "the Laugh Man" Hart. That case of "laryngitis" matches what should be a key developmental milestone for the Tuaoi crystal's internal memory matrix.

I feel bad for Cayce, dancing on this thing's puppet strings, but at least he can talk again.

1943 BCE, JUNE 12: THE SURGEON

Once I figured out which sub it was, it wasn't hard faking up enlistment documents and getting assigned to the USS *R-12*, out of Key West. Officially she's on a training mission, but we're actually sailing straight for Bimini. Classified orders straight out of Washington, very hush-hush. Some secret weapon that could turn the tide of the war effort is "buried under the ocean floor" at a set of coordinates that exactly matches where I found the thing at Bimini.

I snuck a look at the top secret dossier accompanying the orders: definitely something they got from Cayce. My best guess is that someone in his inner circle is working for the War Department. Or at least they have been ever since he first mentioned that death ray.

I can't completely take the death ray out of play. It's part of what got me into this game, so removing it would introduce another layer of paradox. And its absence in 1958 – and more importantly, in 1961 – would tip my hand to Amelia.

But I can blunt its effectiveness.

«later»

I took a few more readings from the Tuaoi Stone while they were drilling, but did nothing more to try to weaken it. I could tell it was growing in power, but other than double-checking the measurements to determine how effective my gambit with the stone circles had been, I did nothing.

If I attack it now, it won't be strong enough in 1968 to send me running, introducing yet another paradox.

THE SURGEON AND OTHERS.

«later»

I scuttled the boat. One of the seals on the forward torpedo tubes "failed" and flooded. I made it to the surface with the commander and the rest of the bridge crew, and, not coincidentally, the proto-cuneiform tablets with the blueprints for a simple high-energy turbolaser.

Not exactly the same plans the War Department is going to receive, of course.

1961 CE, DECEMBER 1: THE SURGEON

The security at this place is abysmal. I could have broken in here with a paperclip and some bubblegum. Admittedly, the Tempus made it easier.

I behold my handiwork: it's a death ray, alright. A death ray that will weigh 30,000 pounds even when it's out of the prototype phase, and can probably only ever be used in space. No game changer in US-Soviet relations. Nikita Khrushchev, you can thank me later.

Martin Marietta still stands to make a few billion in federal defense contracting dollars over the next few decades. I checked. The Lockheed merger still happens in 1995, but without the bump of true Atlantean technology, Martin's not in the driver's seat. So now it's Lockheed Martin instead of Martin Lockheed. Not as precise as my usual work, but I can live with it.

Dr. Kober's going to demo the thing for the press at the big facility in Denver in about a week. I've ensured that it will get big coverage, but not from any trained science writers. It should ensure that none of the reporting is detailed enough for Amelia to know the difference.

I've got the Tempus on autopilot, making jumps all over the place to keep Earhart off my tail while I take care of these little errands, and then going back to make sure I show my face in enough of the same times that she thinks she's still got me boxed in.

1968 CE, MAY 24: THE SURGEON

I didn't even wait to fully materialize before I triggered the neural dampener on the USS *Scorpion*, another US Navy sub, this time sailing out of the Azores. Lights out for everybody but me: all 99 of them.

She's recorded as having disappeared sometime after 21 May 1968, so this shouldn't disturb the timeline too much.

I took my sweet time setting the MEM-tags I'd lifted from the Citadel with Reagan's help – gave the whole crew new, different lives, and I've bribed the memory technicians enough to make them stick – and then activated them all at once, leaving me all alone on a nuclear submarine in the middle of the Cold War.

Just like I wanted.

1968 CE, SEPTEMBER 29: THE SURGEON

The Tuaoi Stone is gone.

I recovered the *Scorpion* about 80 miles from Bimini, resting at low power on a seabed ridge off of most of the major sea-lanes. A few seals had started to give, and she was taking on water, but I wasn't planning for her to survive long, anyway. I spent about two days jury-rigging the controls to run by remote, or at worst with a crew of one.

The Tuaoi Stone was gathering power, set to hit another developmental milestone before it could trigger the full recursion. Disappearances in its field of influence – now with a famous name, the Bermuda Triangle, thanks to *Argosy* magazine – were becoming more common as the tachyon field became less stable, and the thing was tuned in to a whole new population of mouthpieces thanks to Cayce's ceaseless advocacy of resonant crystals 30 years before. None had the same kind of natural connection that Cayce did, but all sorts of people were wearing quartz prisms and preparing for the dawn of a "New Age of Aquarius," and unfortunately they were not wrong.

At least not unless I could take the Tuaoi Stone out of the picture.

I set the *Scorpion*'s navigation for Bimini, and went to work on the reactor. I needed it to stay steady state until it got within transduction range of the crystal, and then I needed the energy-production rate to go through the roof. Quickly.

Once I was satisfied with my efforts as a cut-rate nuclear engineer I jumped out, but stayed in the same time. I needed to make sure my theory was right. I needed to make sure this would work. I needed everything to go like clockwork.

The sensor suite I installed on the *Scorpion* worked great up until the very end. She approached Bimini as planned, and, as predicted, the Tuaoi Stone started siphoning the additional energy right off of the reactor. At operating levels, the reactor wasn't powerful enough to have much effect on the crystal itself, but when she started to overload things got hairy.

As best I can tell, the power from the *Scorpion*'s reactor flooded the Tuaoi Stone with more energy than it could handle, triggering the recursion before it had finished recalculating the quantum field variables to rebuild the timeline Graves destroyed... and then it just disappeared, taking the "Hall of Records" along with it. Poof. Like it was never there. Maybe it never was.

The *Scorpion* went with it – or at least part of it did. The whole center section of the hull, including the reactor, is gone to whatever phantom zone or neverwhere the crystal itself went to. The forward sections of the sub reappeared in the South Atlantic about 600 miles east of Bimini, and the aft decks are at the bottom of an impact trench just off Cozumel.

The whole area is still highly unstable, and it will take local space-time a few eons to repair itself before the Bermuda Triangle is completely safe to travel through again. I can't fix everything Graves screwed up.

But I do still have one thing left to do.

1958 CE, NOVEMBER 16 + 15 MINUTES: THE SURGEON

I ease my way into the alley, taking care to ensure that my past self doesn't see me as he walks out the front door. He's on the way to the library.

I have other business to attend to.

I can just hear her talking into her tether, reporting to her superiors in the Citadel. "... I continue to monitor his progress, and will ensure that there are no loose ends once this is done."

I pad closer, and ease the Centauri particle disruptor out of its shoulder holster.

"Tether, end recording and begin transmission," she says. Cool. Professional. Like she didn't just promise to kill someone. To kill me.

I wait for the tether to answer. It does, in a chirpy synthesized voice, after about 15 seconds. "Transmission complete."

She reaches up to shut it down, probably putting her hands as far away from her weapons as they can be. I'm not taking chances with this.

I thumb the power module on the disruptor. She spins to face me.

"Ah ah! Hands up. Way up. Any sudden moves and you're subatomic vapor," I say. In the moment, I mean it. "Turn that thing back on. Now."

She nods, slowly. "Tether, begin recording."

1958 CE, NOVEMBER 16 + 16 MINUTES: AMELIA EARHART

Begin tether recording.

THE SURGEON AND OTHERS.

REDACTED: You're sure that thing is on? It's recording?

Earhart: I'm sure. Here, you can come check it yourself.

REDACTED: And get clobbered by a PaciFist? I'll keep my distance thankyou-verymuch. Just make sure it's recording. I want your boss back at the Citadel to hear this.

Earhart: I can . . . I . . . I'm not sure what you heard back there, but I'm sure I can explain! It's not what you –

REDACTED: [interrupting] Don't bother.

Earhart: Is it your fee? I assure you that we are willing to negotiate additional terms of service if necessary!

REDACTED: Funny thing about that. I had an old friend of mine check the co-ordinates for my fee. Everything is there, just like I asked for. The money. The painting. The car. There's also a temporal stasis generator and a medium-yield nuclear warhead. Pretty well hidden, too. If I didn't know any better, I'd think you were trying to [threatening] tie up loose ends.

Earhart: [nervous] That's impossible! TimeWatch would never –

REDACTED: [talking over Earhart] Save it. "Never" is meaningless when you literally control time. It's a shame, too. I really, really wanted that car. But really – you don't need to worry about me. I grabbed a few choice items from the Templar treasure on Oak Island for my trouble. Maybe more than a few items. [pause] Basically all of it.

Earhart: What does that have to do with me?

REDACTED: Just wanted your bosses to know I consider this matter closed. No more side jobs. No more contact. I'm out of the game. For good this time . . . and if they decide to reach out? Well, I start spreading the word about where all your little toys come from.

THE SURGEON AND OTHERS.

Earhart: You mean the Citadel?

REDACTED: I mean where they came from originally. See, it took me a long time to figure out why there was so much Atlantis still left around after Graves excised it from the core timeline. He's sloppy. Careless. Too stupid to see any of the truth himself, yeah. But nobody's this bad. Not even him.

Honestly, it wasn't until I got a good look at one of the big crystals that I was sure: the Atlanteans weren't using stolen TimeWatch gear. TimeWatch stole it from them! That's why you were so hot to cover this up. That's why this all had to be done by deniable assets. Freelancers and fools.

Tell me the truth, Amelia: how long had the war been going on before you decided to stop it at its source? Millennia? Eons? Eternity?

Earhart: Even if that were true, how would you prove it? To whom?

REDACTED: Prove it!? I don't have to prove it. TimeWatch has enough enemies, I just have to start the rumor. But I won't. Not unless you cross me again. I'm even going to let you live. [muttered] Against my better judgment.

Earhart: [quietly] They won't let you get away with this. I . . . I'm sorry, but they won't take threats like these. This won't end well. Not for either of us.

REDACTED: I really can't speak for you, but I'm going to get out of this just fine. See, I've got one other ace up my sleeve. See, Graves really *is* sloppy. That Atlantean leader he thought was a rebel? The one he left in orbital chrono-stasis? See, I've got him. Hidden away a little pocket universe of my own devising. And if I ever – *ever* – see you, or any other TimeWatch flunky again? I let him go, and start your little eternity war all over again. Are we clear?

Earhart: We're . . . clear.

REDACTED: Good. Good day, Ms. Earhart. [shouted] Tether, end recording and begin transmission!

End tether recording. Begin Transmission.

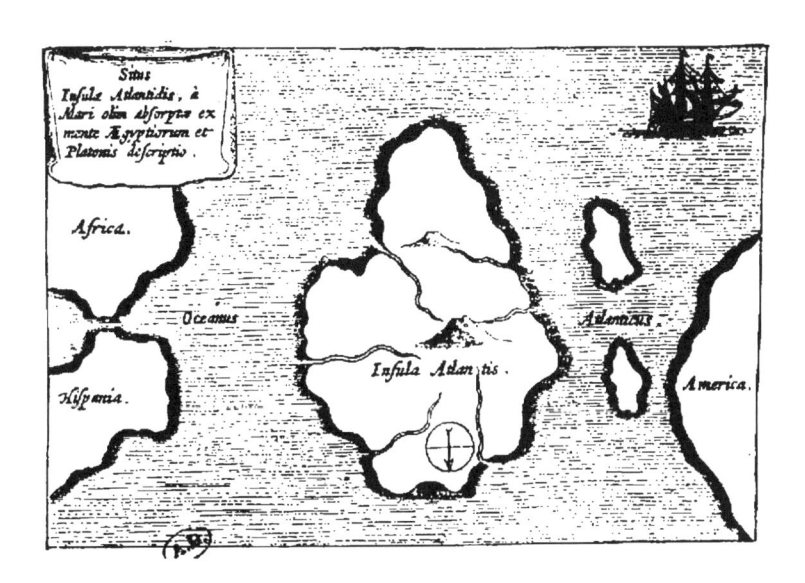

SITUS INSULAE ATLANTIDIS, A MARI OLIM ABSORPTE EX MENTE AEGYPTIORUM ET PLATONIS DESCRIPTIO.

FROM *MUNDUS SUBTERRANEUS*,
ATHANASIUS KIRCHER, AMSTERDAM 1665.
SOEMONE ALWAYS REMEMBERS.

TEMPLETON GRAVES.

JOURNAL OF PUBLIA DECIA SUBULO.

PUBLIA DECIA SUBULO.
47 CE –

JOURNAL OF PUBLIA DECIA SUBULO.

1840 CE
London.

Team arrived in London on patrol duty for the Convention of London. Rex-94 immediately alerted us to the unusually high numbers of cats and lack of dogs. We observed cats entering places of business and state buildings, as well as family homes. Most persons had at least one cat constantly at their side. Seven or eight might leap out of a coach alongside a family. Despite my time living in Egypt, where cats were treasured and deified, this is far outside my experience.

«later»

Rex-94 successfully disguised himself as a cat, though he was not at all pleased with the situation. He spent the afternoon gathering blood samples from a cross section of the London population. Upon returning, he expressed disgust at how little these humans protested the scratches which should at least have inspired a "naughty puss!" Cats gave him more trouble by refusing to accept his disguise. José acquired the cat samples with little difficulty, though he found the cats' friendly pliancy unsettling.

Min, Tesfaye, and I visited the British Museum and its library to look for other obvious changes. We found the place swarming with cats. Tesfaye and I briefly surveyed the art for changes while Min visited the library's maps department. While art is neither of our specialties, we were overwhelmed by the sheer number of cat paintings and cats in sculpture. Some of the art represents lions and tigers in traditional English scenes, sprawling at picnics or sitting proudly in drawing rooms. Min reports the basic geography and country borders check out, but she found numerous pyramids in new locations, including some inhabited by non-pyramid-building cultures. She also noted that the famous pyramids properly found in Giza are now farther south upstream, around the Third Cataract. A consultation of the library's reference material confirms that they were still built by the same pharaohs.

«later»

Rex-94 and José declared the blood samples normal except for a 100% toxoplasmosis infection rate among both cats and humans. They conducted soil tests, as well, and found an abnormally high level of toxoplasma oocysts. The strain of toxoplasmosis is greatly evolved beyond what has been seen on Earth, even into the 4th millennium.

Min cataloged the new and differently located pyramids for further inspection. In particular, she found that all new instances of pyramids occur between the Tropics of Cancer and Capricorn. Sub-Saharan Africa's pyramids follow the Nile, Congo, and Niger. Lake Victoria and the Congo Delta are each dotted with around a dozen pyramids. Similarly, the pre-Columbian Amazonians erected step pyramids in the style of the Maya to their north. The Pacific island of Borneo only contains a single pyramid in its southwest quadrant. Australia is surprisingly pyramid free. The greatest period of activity occurred between 600 and 700 BCE.

After calling in a few favors, I've arranged for coverage at the convention while we investigate further.

648 CE
Lake Victoria, Nalubaale, southern edge.

All of us except Min & Rex-94 disguised ourselves as workers to infiltrate the site of the second Nalubaale pyramid. Again, the area is overrun with cats, which the workers treat with a casual affection. I was particularly surprised by the family of cheetahs which have the run of the place. Rex-94 grudgingly accepted his duty and is on sample rotation again. The rest of us are searching for external influences. While TimeWatch has debunked the "ancient aliens" Anunnaki theory, it is entirely possible that the ezeru, reptoids, or a time traveler may be involved here.

Min spent the day with the foreman, disguised as a former Egyptian-Byzantine architect who fled after the Byzantines' recent defeat by the Caliphate. She learned from him that, unlike the Egyptians who built pyramids in Kush, they do not erect these to honor dead god-kings. They are not tombs at all, but solid structures: "teats of the fertility goddess." The foreman seemed surprised she had not heard of the great blessings in Kush – fertile soil around the Nile's Third Cataract, extending far into the desert. He told her that their own goddess had blessed them after the completion of the first structure. Crops had increased fourfold that year.

Min asked if anything else had changed during that time or if they had been visited by outsiders or manifestations of the gods. Apparently the number of cats had greatly increased, and formerly wild felines began to live among them. He explained this as a consequence of the population increase among birds and rodents which fed on the harvest. The cats were a blessing, he said, sent to protect the food for humans.

«later»

Tesfaye and Min traveled to the completed pyramid to scan it for anomalies and discovered a strong magnetic field. It had a strong north-northeastern pull and a weaker west-northwestern one. Is it possible that these structures are interfering with Earth's magnetic field? After Min advised us of the region's fruitful harvest, José confirmed from the samples that, besides the presence of oocysts, the soil is far more fertile than previous records indicate. He tested the oocysts for a possible connection but found none. We need an era with a more comprehensive data set. As expected, Rex-94 reports a 100% toxoplasmosis infection rate. José says the parasite has not evolved as far as we saw in 1840 CE, but it is still more stable than that of our day.

2089 CE
Columbia University, New York City.

On Min's suggestion, we visited the Columbia-based Goddard Institute for Space Studies, which collects and analyzes satellite data about Earth and its habitability. Min immediately noticed differences in the data compared to her time there about 75 years later. She remarked on the complete lack of global warming. While Earth's temperature still naturally fluctuated, data from approximately 750 CE forward shows relatively stable conditions and a sudden improvement in agriculture worldwide. Population has self-regulated as it so often does among prosperous nations, so that the world's population is approximately what it should have been.

Min had the bright idea of taking two graduate students out to a nice dinner and asking them about their work. They were more than happy to talk about their passions on someone else's coin. Saffiya and Ralph study anthropogenic architecture and its effect on Earth's magnetic fields. Human pyramid-building activity has been Earth's greatest blessing, but until the invention of satellites in the mid-20th century, no one had been able to determine why. Ralph studies the sun's effect on the magnetosphere, with a particular focus on how the magnetic fields have stabilized due to pyramidal influence. Saffiya is writing her doctoral thesis on theoretical models of pyramid-building outside the tropical zone. From her we confirmed that, had the Great Pyramid of Khufu and its companions been built north of the Tropic of Cancer, subsequent building activity would not have affected the magnetosphere. Despite the Egyptians building their great pyramids around

2500 BCE, the effect required a second spate of activity in the Maya civilization half a world away.

While we interviewed the students, Tesfaye and José visited the New York Public Library. The greatest change they found beyond the agricultural prosperity we had already discovered was a complete absence of major rodent-borne diseases, such as the Black Death. When Tesfaye asked in particular about plague rats, the cat-sweatered librarian seemed amused by the idea. Rats hadn't been a problem for over a thousand years, although many people bred them as food for their cats. José consulted medical literature on toxoplasmosis, which is considered as benign as our other intestinal flora. He did not find any references to what we would consider "acute" stages of toxoplasmosis.

José believes there must be a connection here, as the parasite *Toxoplasma gondii* can only reproduce in cat intestines. It affects infected prey animals such as rodents by reducing their natural repulsion to feline predator odors. Once the rodents are consumed, the oocysts generated in the cat's intestines are spread through fecal matter ingested by humans, rodents, and other animals. The parasite then thrives in human systems without necessarily causing complications. Infected humans are more likely to continue association with cats and risk reinfection.

In the 20th century, this cycle was often called "crazy cat lady syndrome." This evolved form of the parasite is no longer harmful to its human hosts and, indeed, seems to have cemented a mutually beneficial symbiotic relationship with cats. What then of the pyramid connection? In our timeline, biologists suspect *Toxoplasma gondii* may have a reduced hivemind capability. They are evidently capable of influencing their hosts to take actions, even actions against their best interests. How much easier would it be for them to convince their hosts to take an action that is, at best, beneficial and, at worst, neutral to their well-being as a species?

Rex-94 reports a complete absence of dogs in the city. As team leader, I may recommend he receive a psychological evaluation after we complete our mission. At least his chronal stability is unaffected.

637 CE
Yucatan Peninsula.

Just a short visit. Saffiya estimates this as the year when Yucatan pyramids reached a critical mass to affect the magnetosphere, despite their comparatively small size when compared to those in Kush. Rex-94 has found a toxoplasmosis infection rate of only 85%.

Jaguars roam as freely as housecats. I witnessed multiple builders feeding the great cats with bits of roasted flesh. The jaguar is a revered animal to the Maya, associated with royalty, fertility, and a plentiful harvest. The builders consider it a sign of good fortune that these animals have become so familiar. Nothing in our records, however, indicates such cohabitation between jaguars and humans in the Maya civilization.

None of us detected outside interference, though we did find a strong magnetic pull between the completed pyramids and what we surmise to be the pyramid of Khufu. From what we can tell, this stop is the closest we've come to encountering historical normalcy.

2555 BCE
Third Cataract of the Nile, Kush.

Only the base of Khufu's pyramid is complete so far. Rather than quarry at Aswan, the Egyptians chose to use stone from a site approximately 20 km upstream. Min found no fundamental difference between these granite and limestone blocks and those which would have been brought from Aswan. From Saffiya's research, she deduces that the location of the pyramid matters more than its building materials.

Tesfaye, posing as an Ethiopian trader from the south, entered the camp of the Egyptian traders who supply the necessities to keep the workers clothed and fed. He inquired why the Egyptians had chosen to build a burial place for their god-kings in Kush, rather than somewhere closer to the capital at Memphis. The traders attributed it to the coming of a white prophet whose magic had dazzled Khufu's court. The man had arrived in the third year of Khufu's reign, at the time of the cattle count, and become indispensable to the king. He could conjure music from the air and had accurately predicted the inundations since his arrival, ensuring adequate preparation for lean seasons. He referred to himself as the one who prepared the way for the chariots of the gods. He predicted that beings from across the stars would soon arrive and provide guidance to Pharaoh. (The phrase, "chariots of the gods" appears in TimeWatch's database conjoined with some of the earliest references to "ancient astronauts.") This man prophesied that Khufu's legacy would endure forever if only he were to build his tomb at the Nile's Third Cataract. After some trade negotiations, Khufu's chief architect secured permission from the Kushites to build here.

JOURNAL OF PUBLIA DECIA SUBULO.

2586 BCE, SECOND DAY OF THE CATTLE COUNT
Memphis, Egypt.

Since this man makes no effort to disguise his race, we traveled to the first day of the cattle count and stationed ourselves to look for a white man. As the most unobtrusive, I would approach and attempt to detect whether he were of this time and place or the man we sought. I scanned a few Greeks the first day, but this morning José gave the signal and I identified a rather nervous character as our man. Then came the challenge of intercepting him.

This proved easier than expected. Min proposed it; the "ancient astronaut" theory was one of her peeves during graduate school. We simply approached the man and represented ourselves as ancient astronauts, here to ensure the proper construction of the pyramids. He animatedly introduced himself as Philip Jones, a geologist who'd come all the way from 2084 CE to meet us. He showed us his notes and maps, explaining that he'd been studying the placement of pyramids and Earth's geography. Had we considered having the Egyptians build in the tropical zone? It would make the spread of pyramids properly balanced and, he calculated, significantly improve the planet's magnetosphere, encouraging harvests. When we asked what he'd used to dazzle the court, he sheepishly showed us an electronic music device with speakers and solar battery and a small book of Egyptian inundation records corresponding to this period.

Tesfaye, always the master of bullshit, gave him a stern explanation of why, if the pyramids were built anywhere but Giza, the world would end in 2012 CE. He asked Jones if he'd never heard of the Mayan calendar and wondered why the world hadn't ended as it predicted (José had a hard time not laughing). Our work was to preserve this fragile species we had created by balancing the tectonic forces at the core of this planet. Did Jones truly understand the delicate balance of the planet's core? He thought not. He impressed on Jones our need for subtlety in influencing these earthlings, thanked him for his efforts to assist, and charged him to keep everything we had revealed a secret. Tesfaye will escort him back to his own time to ensure his safe arrival. I've given instructions to lightly alter Jones' memory after arrival so he believes he had an alien visitation in his own time and remove the time travel device to keep him from messing around again.

JOURNAL OF PUBLIA DECIA SUBULO.

TIMEWATCH HQ

Debriefed concerning our action. We are left pondering the operation and its significance. Could it be that toxoplasmosis, as a hivemind, desired the environment Jones unwittingly effected? Did it have a collective awareness of the geographical conditions in which it lived and seek to affect them in a way that benefited its hosts and itself? A humanity free from famine is a stronger humanity which can tolerate higher infection rates. A humanity with higher infection rates has a stronger affection for the cats which breed it. Thus the cycle of infection is perpetuated, but once the parasite evolves beyond damaging humans, is it really a parasite anymore? Its failure might be attributed to an incomplete level of evolution, which led to the right action being performed but 10 degrees north of where it would have an effect. As an agent, I am bound to the code and must protect the timeline, even from changes I perceive as beneficial. But I am left asking – if Kushites instead of Egyptians had been cat devotees, would we all have lived on a better planet?

end

LAKE VICTORIA WITH STEPPED PYRAMIDS
SIMILAR TO THOSE AT SAKKARA.

MARRIAGE *A LA MODE*, THE TÊTE À TÊTE
BY WILLIAM HOGARTH, 1743.

JOURNAL OF ENGINEER PRITESH.

ENGINEER PRITESH.
1883 CE –

JOURNAL OF ENGINEER PRITESH.

1986 CE, JANUARY 28

Our new recruit is ill, and we can't get back to the Citadel. We had just completed the Challenger mission and had our new recruit ready to go. I put the coordinates into the autochron, but something odd is happening. Was that alligator rabid, or were we standing too close to the river? Either way she was bit, and her leg already seems infected.

Worse, we can't even take her back to the Citadel. The autochrons keep slipping up whenever I try to program them – they're either on the fritz, or it's possible they're deliberately keeping us out. We'll shoot for the near future instead.

2012 CE, APRIL 15

It's as I feared. Humanity is gone. Our long reign is over, and just 26 years after we strapped seven humans to a rocket to launch them into space. Sure, that rocket blew up, thanks to our agents' efforts. But it's not as if anyone died, and stopping that madman was necessary.

«later»

We have to get out of here. There's a horde of them outside. They look human, but ... they're definitely not in their own minds. And they just keep coming. I'm trying to get the autochrons to sync up, but we've all agreed to meet back a day after we left. Hopefully Dr. Okafor can stabilize Chrissy in our absence.

1986 CE, JANUARY 29

My autochron worked, as did Ace's. Eloise took a detour to 17th-century France, but I think she just wanted a baguette.

Chrissy's condition worsened overnight. Dr. Okafor is stymied and wants to take her to a time when we can have her treated without triggering the world's greatest mystery. Right now, we can't even take her to a hospital without triggering a headline like "Hope restored: Challenger astronauts walk into health clinic."

Speaking of headlines, Ace showed me a magazine he retrieved from an abandoned beauty shop in 2012. It's about three years old, talks about the "ZPlague" and "Patient Zero." No identity on Patient Zero, but there's a reference to the disease reaching the United States sometime in the 1980s.

JOURNAL OF ENGINEER PRITESH.

1986 CE, JANUARY 30

Chrissy has died.

She got very still – I was sure she'd died, though Dr. Okafor said she was still breathing, though labored. But then something happened to her. She lurched towards us, nearly foaming at the mouth like a rabid animal.

Ace put her down with his Smith & Wesson. I'm not sure how I feel about that, but it's clear that whatever was behind those eyes, it was no longer the funny, brave teacher we all came to know during our mission, the woman we decided to save from the disaster and take with us to the Citadel.

No, that woman was gone, and what was left was a mindless creature, bent on violence.

1862 CE, FEBRUARY 17

Ace keeps a cabin on the California-Nevada border where we're holing up while Dr. Okafor runs some experiments. It's not ideal, but Okafor's lab won't be built for another 300 years – well after the end of humanity in this time stream.

«later»

Okafor just handed us the bad news. Chrissy's samples are positive for Colony spores. I'm not sure how we're not all infected. Certainly, the horde we saw in 2012 didn't act like mind-controlled mold-carriers. I sincerely hope this isn't a mutation – we all just got the new vaccination!

1986 CE, JANUARY 27

We're back in the Florida swamp. About fifty miles away, we're also doing our last training checks and talking to the press about what we want to have for dinner tonight. The sun is close to setting, which works to our advantage, since if anyone sees us, we don't want them to see the astronauts whose faces are all over the newspapers this week.

We found a black pickup truck on the side of the road, door open, keys on the ground. There's . . . a lot of blood. Ace popped back a few hours and saw two men, one of them sick. The sick one bit the driver, and they both stumbled out into the swamp. He tracked them in the swamp, but lost the trail when a couple of alligators nearly attacked him.

Okay, maybe dusk isn't the right time to go poking around an alligator-infested swamp.

2009 CE, NOVEMBER 11

Observational work is tedious, but I'm pretty good at it, and Eloise isn't a bad companion. We've set up an observation site inside the Met, but it's been rough going. We're watching the infected. I know they're supposedly Colonized, but they don't act like it – they're just shuffling around until they perceive something ... or someone ... they view as prey.

I don't want to describe what we've seen. It was ... bad. A stray cat ... a squirrel. As soon as they were bit, they convulsed, then began their rabid shuffling, too. When we saw the school bus ...Eloise left. I had to finish recording, and I will remember their voices until I die.

1862 CE, FEBRUARY 18

I brought the recordings back to Dr. Okafor. I'm afraid I was a bit brusque with him, but I don't care.

We know now that the ZPlague is a mutated strain of Colony that, blessedly, isn't psychically linked to the main Colony host. That's great, and it transmits via bite, which I guess is why they named it "ZPlague."

Thankfully, we don't have to go back. When she left, Eloise went to the museum's employee break room and found a newspaper that hinted at Patient Zero's identity, but for privacy reasons would still not reveal it. Apparently, he was a Russian athlete in the 1984 Olympics.

There were no Russians in the 1984 Olympics, though that seems like a trivial detail compared to the death of all non-Colony life on Earth!

1984 CE, JULY 21

What a difference Los Angeles is, compared to the nightmare we've been in for the past several jumps! Pennants flapping in the wind, flags of every country – I think Dr. Okafor actually teared up when he saw the Nigerian flag hanging along Santa Monica Boulevard.

As sentimental as this is, there is work to be done. The outbreak started here,

JOURNAL OF ENGINEER PRITESH.

during the Olympics. We have one week to find Patient Zero.

1984 CE, JULY 28

The opening ceremonies were very moving. Eloise made contact with an older Russian couple, here to watch the games.

«later»

Eloise made us take the Russians to dinner, where Ace plied the husband, Alexi, with vodka, and Eloise put her charms to the test with Ingva. Ingva's brother works in a military facility in Aldan, a small village in Siberia. She claims half the Russian gymnastics team is there "recovering from illness," and the entire team almost skipped the Olympics.

"No one goes to Siberia to recover, *da*?"

Ominous words. We're going to Aldan.

1985 CE, NOVEMBER 25

I think we overshot our destination, but it does not seem to have made much difference. Aldan is a cold, desolate place. The military facility is an underground complex that was once a mine and labor camp. Now, it's a nondescript bunker with two young soldiers standing guard.

«later»

The guards let us in. We've located the central computer. This thing is freakishly old. Ace and Dr. Okafor are on guard duty while I try to get an interface set up.

«later»

Downloaded the surveillance videos. Given what we saw on them ... We have to go in.

«later»

Dr. Okafor's been hurt – bad burns on his left arm from the flamethrower. I feel like shit – I didn't even see him! There was so much smoke and those things – it was dark! I didn't know he was there. I didn't know...

I feel like shit, and I'm making excuses.

There were dozens of them in the central science lab. Ace tried to lay down a blanket of fire to keep them at bay, but there were so many. Patients, military, doctors – all Infected, their eyes glazed over, their hands clawing at us. We'd evaded some in the hallways... killed a few there, if we're honest. But the main lab was the central hot spot for the infection.

Dr. Okafor wanted to get into Quarantine Cell 5, the "hot quarantine": the one we think has Patient Zero in it, or as close to Patient Zero as we might get. I worked on the door while Ace kept the flamethrower handy. I don't know what drew him away – I was paying more attention to the door. But the next thing I know, I'm holding a flamethrower while trying to use a badly secured keypad from the 1960s one handed.

I didn't see Okafor approach – just a shadow coming towards me from the darkness. And all the Infected look alike.

1985 CE, NOVEMBER 25
later that day: Eloise Poirot.

Eloise here. Pritesh is momentarily indisposed. After we got Dr. Okafor to safety, Ace and Prit opened the quarantine cells. I've taken the liberty of attaching photos of the patients we encountered to this log entry. It should be fairly clear that the man inside Quarantine Cell 3 – a man who has been there for roughly twenty years, from what we can tell – is a TimeWatch agent. He also seems quite insane, and I can only conjecture what twenty years of solitary in a Soviet gulag might have done to this poor man.

I've met Jack Orleans once before. He bought me a drink in Madagascar in 1939, as I recall. Well, I can safely report he is much worse for the wear.

The ... person in Quarantine Cell 5 is much more troubling, of course. I've attached the photos we were able to snap before we realized what we were looking at. Despite the vapor cloud, I think one can clearly see signs of Colony infection covering this man – and the eyes are of course a dead giveaway. We shut the door as soon as we realized it was Colony, but we've decided not to leave this facility until we're convinced we won't be taking spores with us.

JOURNAL OF ENGINEER PRITESH.

1961 CE, FEBRUARY 10

We're still in Aldan, this hellish gulag. I have the cracked password for their central computer system, and as luck would have it, they haven't changed protocols in the next twenty years. Thank you, Soviet Russia! The surveillance recordings from this period were all damaged, but we did find at least one "incident" from this date, so we picked it for our investigation.

«later»

Quarantine 5 was breached. We have to run. Now.

1961 CE, AUGUST 10

Shit. I hit the panic switch and transported to six months later. At least they have the outbreak contained again. This is such a mess. No idea where Ace and Eloise and the doctor ended up – I hope Dr. Okafor made it back to the Citadel and isn't in the 16th century, looking for a burn unit.

I also saw that the Aldan lab has been burn-sanitized, and Quarantine 5 is back in his cell. How did he survive all that? I have no idea – the Colony is resilient. I'll slide forward and see what's changed.

1963 CE, JANUARY 10

I poked my head out for air and saw that they were booking Jack Orleans into Quarantine Cell 3 – poor man has no idea what's going on. I snuck into the lab to ask him a few questions; he says he was captured at the Bay of Pigs in Cuba. Cuba?

He reports that he succeeded in his part, and the ezeru didn't force World War III to happen. "Everything since then has been a nightmare, though," he tells me. Some of the other prisoners became Infected, one of them acting like the thing in the swamp that bit Chrissy; they were evacuated to the US anyway in the prisoner exchange last year. He alone seems to have survived unharmed, and has since been transferred here. His autochron was confiscated by someone wearing a Cuban uniform but speaking Russian.

I wonder if Jack is immune due to the vaccinations we all receive at the Citadel. If so, then my team should be safe enough. I didn't have the heart to tell Jack how long he's going to be here, so I told him I have an older autochron that can't take additional people.

Since it's been more than a day with no growth, I'm fairly confident my uniform has repelled the spores. I'm willing to try jumping back to Ace's cabin.

1863 CE, JUNE 5

I found Dr. Okafor and Ace. Eloise is still missing in the time stream, but I expect her to show up here soon. Or possibly yesterday – who knows. We can't get Okafor to the Citadel yet, and we can't treat him here. I think we might have to leave him behind until we have the time stream almost sorted out. He objects, and rightly so – facing the Colony without our medical officer is ill advised, at best.

1962 CE, DECEMBER 24

We're in the Red Cross tents at Havana, and missing Dr. Okafor keenly. Between the normal illnesses you expect in a crowd of men who haven't been treated very well, we've identified three patients – all in restraints – who are showing signs of ZPlague. Ace suggests we can burn the entire tent down to be safe, but Eloise says that will just exacerbate a very tense situation between America and Cuba. Apparently, this is a turning point in not having the Southern United States turn into an ezeru breeding ground. We're sure there are ezeru in the Cuban ranks; we just can't deal with that problem right now.

Jack told me about the places he'd visited during his mission. We're paying a visit to the cigar district next.

«later»

Whatever gods my ancestors held dear would be horrified. They had this weird Santeria shrine in the back of the shop, covered in Colony – I think they were worshipping the spores? I don't know – it certainly gave me the chills! We burned it, all of it – half the district, really – to get rid of the spores and the Infected. I almost felt bad, but not enough to risk the future we saw before. Eloise jumped back to get Dr. Okafor, and we're heading home."

end

THE ALTAR AT THE CIGAR SHOP.

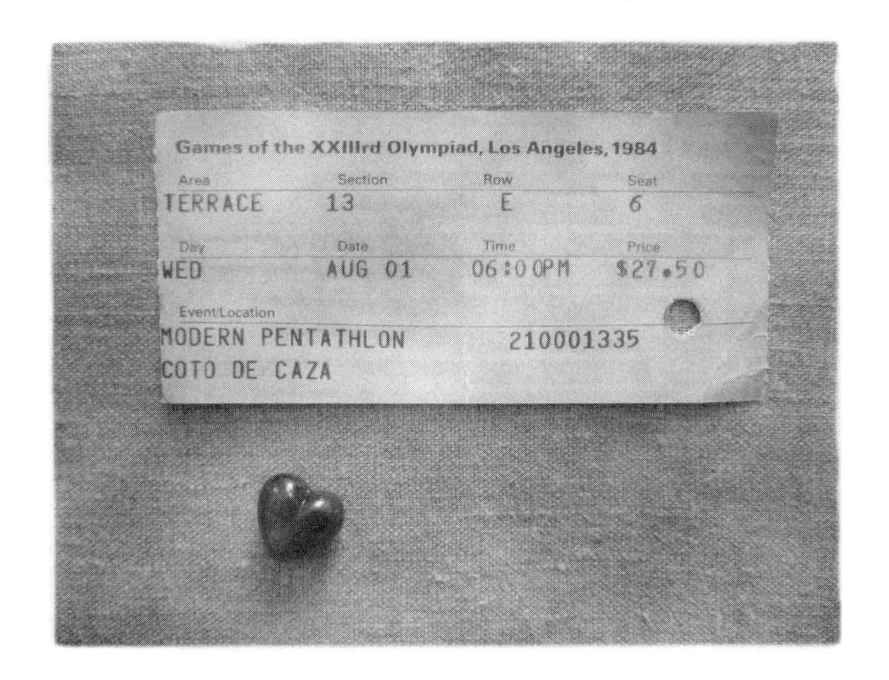

ENGINEER PRITESH.

JOURNAL OF JACOB MOYER.

JACOB MOYER.

1901 CE –

JOURNAL OF JACOB MOYER.

1820 CE
Salem, New Jersey, USA, outside the wretched abode of one
Colonel Robert Gibbon Johnson, around 10 or 11 p. m.

Ah, the waiting. The everlasting moments spent huddling in the dank and dark. It is one of my life's greatest ironies that punctuality is a function of perception and not a function of actual time. Some reprobate is loose in the time stream, with nefarious intent, and the most accurate, the single most surgically precise response we can muster is to drop in a hapless agent hours ahead of schedule just to ensure we don't miss our window of opportunity. So here I sit, in the cold and the mud, waiting for some gourmand with a tomato allergy to show up and poison a bushel of wolf peaches.

And why does the past always smell like laundry left in the closet for too long? I could be lying in a field of wildflowers, in what would otherwise be a picture-perfect fabric softener commercial, and all I'd smell is the stale stench of history. It doesn't even make sense. The world is younger! Shouldn't it smell fresher?

247 BCE
Aboard a Carthaginian warship bound for Sicily on a distressing sea.

I can puke no more. I've puked all I've got and then some. My arms, as sore as they are from all the rowing, and my butt, as sore as it is from the unforgiving bench that I bounce upon as the sea thrashes about, do not ache as much as my guts after the endless hours of dry heaves. I was made to travel in time, not upon the sea.

I'm unsure of what I have followed here, but I have an inkling as to its designs. The "ghost" appears human in all respects. Actually, in more respects than most. It is so unobtrusive that none really notice it. It's hard to see, not because it is transparent, but your mind sort of shoves it to the background. It appears to be so ordinary that your gaze is constantly passing over it as it would pass over any unremarkable tree in a forest. It's so hard to focus on. The only clue that betrays it is the gooseflesh it gives you if you stand too close to it. It feels as if you brushed up against a ghost.

I suspect, given its presence on this very ship at this very moment, that it wishes ill on Hamilcar Barca, who rides with us to Sicily to face the might of the Roman legions. I just do not know why.

JOURNAL OF JACOB MOYER.

1880 CE
In an orchard in Peru, Iowa.

Every agent has their Hitler moment, when they must stand in defense of one of history's greatest monsters and oppose well-intentioned, good people who seek only to save the world from an evil whose sole justification is it happened. Tonight, I had this moment when I tackled a woman in an orchard who was armed with a half-full gas can, a Zippo lighter, and a dream of a world free from the mealy tyranny of the Red Delicious apple. Never have I been more tempted to shirk my duties and light the flames of justice. May I never be so tested again.

20 CE
In some bug-infested swamp in Iceni, Roman occupied Britannia.

Insects, insects, insects. Getting your vaccinations and not drinking the water saves you from the direst discomforts of time travel. But there is no defense against the incessant and unholy omnipresence of insects. They are your constant companions in the past, and the further back you go, the more there are.

I met my ghost friend today. Completely by accident. Brushed up against it, got the goose bumps, and something reminded me of that Carthaginian boat trip to Sicily.

It slipped right past me and into the market crowd, where I lost it on account of its ability to be astoundingly unremarkable. This has me a bit worried. If I had dealt with it back in the BCE, then we're earlier in its timeline, which probably means I won't be terribly successful here.

Or worse yet, it could mean there's more than one.

So that's the bad news. The good news is, I'm starting to see a pattern. My ghost friend may be after some of the more famous enemies of Rome. We're here a few years early for Boudica, but just about right on time to do her parents in, if that's its intent. Here's hoping I can find it first.

1972 CE
Phoenix, Arizona.

Just used my PaciFist on some old bald dude with a copy of *D&D* that's not supposed to be in print for another year. He was trying to sneak it into a game store. Apparently the plan was to casually place it in Ken St. Andre's path so that he'd read it and be inspired to create *Tunnels & Trolls* a few years ahead of schedule, making it the first ever roleplaying game. The bald dude was vehement about vanquishing initiative orders and separate damage rolls from his hobby once and for all. What is it with nerds and time travel? What kind of monster looks upon such a profound opportunity and thinks of such frivolous abuses for it?

1158 CE
Along the banks of the Onon River.

It's my ghost friend again. This time, I'm onto it. No more than 200 m. to the west of here sleeps Qaban, who will soon become the father of Jelme and then Subutai, two of Genghis Kahn's mighty dogs of war. At first I thought it was trying to rewrite some Roman history by removing Rome's greatest enemies before they were even born. But now I see this ghost has a thing for the parents of generals in general.

I haven't quite narrowed down the why of it, but now that I know the what, it's going to be a bit easier to stop. I just have to keep an eye on Qaban and wait for something completely unremarkable to happen. All right, not entirely easy, yet, but easier. I've dealt with it twice before. I can deal with it again.

1936 CE
Whitman, Massachusetts.

Today, I love my job.

Today, I apprehended a man who traveled eighty years back in time to steal a bunch of chocolate from an inn. A man who was attempting to delay a fundamental culinary advance by eighty years so that he could take the credit for it when he became a finalist on "The Great American Bake Off" season two.

Today, I was caught in the act of doing my duty by the warm and generous woman who runs this inn. To thank me, she baked me something using the very chocolate I saved.

Today, I had the distinct pleasure of being the very first person ever to eat a chocolate chip cookie. While it was still warm and all melty from the oven. The very first chocolate chip cookie.

Today, I love my job.

JOURNAL OF JACOB MOYER.

9430 BCE
In a box canyon, hiding between the ice boulders.

I have been numb for a while now, but an intense warmth is inexplicably flooding back into my limbs. I know this to be a sign of hypothermia, but I will not move. Not until I can be sure it's safe.

The ghosts were here.

I do not know how many. More than one, certainly. Perhaps more than a dozen. Perhaps they numbered in the thousands. It's impossible to tell. I stood in a crowd of them in this very valley for I don't know how long before it ever occurred to me that the *Homo erectus* of the late Pleistocene did not carry firearms. The cold masked the telltale goose pimples.

I fled and hid.

And then I tried to focus. I tried to keep my mind on them. To see them for the aberrations that they are, but my brain just wouldn't let me. I just kept seeing them as something so utterly and completely mundane that my eyes just swept over them as if they were single blades of grass in a giant field.

And then the massacre began. A massive stampede of mastodons was funneled into the canyon. There they were gunned down. Hundreds of them. Maybe even thousands. The awful cries of the dying beasts echoing off of the glacial walls. To what end? What horrifying purpose could this possibly serve?

2024 CE
Cleveland, Ohio, one week until the NFL draft.

Millions of dollars are collectively spent each year by professional sports teams on complex statistical analysis and deep computer simulations in an attempt to make the most optimal choices in the draft. Athletes are poked, prodded, tested, and retested. Their home lives and personal history are sifted through by experts and pundits alike. Who is the most athletic? Who has the strongest arm? Who has the right attitude? Who is the best fit for the current team? Who will peak at the right moment?

Millions of dollars, and it's all still so much alchemy. Each year they get fractions of a percent better at guessing an athlete's worth to the team. Each fractional improvement costs more than the last. It's the game within the game within the game. And the stakes have never been higher. Everyone wants to be the next Billy Beane.

All that sweat, toil, and cash, and it still boils down to just a throw of the dice.

Today, the Cleveland Browns are taking a chance on the brainchild of three college sophomores – a computer simulation they're calling the Eventuality Engine. It takes the current state of the league and measures each draft option's possible effectiveness within your team for up to three whole seasons into the future. But it doesn't stop there. It takes into account projected changes to the weather, the socioeconomic climate, and even fan responses to potential controversies that the draft pick may find themselves in. And it does it all in real time, allowing team owners and managers to update the simulation with each pick made by the opposing teams as the draft happens. It is about to demonstrate predictive modeling on a scale and breadth that surpasses anything that has come before by orders of magnitude.

It is a lie and a crime against nature.

The Eventuality Engine does no such modeling. There are simply too many variables for any computer to predict anything that complex with any amount of certainty more than a day or two into the future. Instead, the Eventuality Engine briefly creates unrealized futures based on the parameters fed to it, downloads the next three years of football statistics from that reality's Internet, and then collapses the reality when it is done with it. Wash, rinse, repeat.

The problem is, over the course of three years, a simple change like choosing this tight end over that wide receiver can lead to more than just games won and lost. People meet at games and Super Bowl parties. Alcohol and the natural elation of a shared victory are just the sort of social lubrication needed to create new human life that might never have happened if the wrong player was drafted. And as thousands of these realities are created and collapsed over the course of a single draft, millions of unrealized beings are born within the same three-year span.

These ghosts do not drift quietly into oblivion. They watch our reality with a hunger. They slip in among us, unnoticed and unremarked upon, because were it not for one small choice, they would be us. They travel through time seeking out the parents of important thinkers, leaders, and warriors to prevent them from meeting so that these key individuals will also join the ranks of the unrealized. They are amassing an army of ghosts.

This may be the moment they can be stopped – the day the Eventuality Engine ignites this inferno. And the ghosts know it. Today the streets of Cleveland are choked with unrealized warriors from all of human history mounted upon the backs of mastodons. The power of these ghosts to remain unobtrusive is so compelling that no one notices the spectacle. To the average Clevelander, this is a day like any other. Even I have to keep reminding myself that mastodons are extinct, and I witnessed the horror of their extinction firsthand.

I must stop the Cleveland Browns.

end

JOURNAL OF LIU FEIYAN.

LIU FEYAN.

1858 CE –

JOURNAL OF LIU FEIYAN.

4507 CE
Amundscott, Antarctica

This was a hard one for me. I'm still not used to learning so much about how things go wrong on Earth. We pulled chocks in the city of Amundscott before the impact of the meteorite. We were in plenty of time to rescue many of the Epiterrans, but I can't believe that these really are the last humans to live on the surface of the planet. In my orientation they showed us strips of the devastation sustained by the sea colonies, but it's nothing compared to the destruction of this last outpost of surface human habitation.

«later»

I was taken for an Abyssal by a young woman with midnight-blue hair. She escaped from me, and I wasn't able to find her again. Our request for bilocation was denied. Too much risk of contamination of the site, they said.

«later»

The relocation has gone very well. We're reintroducing some of the chronal refugees into earlier populations. Those we found were either susceptible to suggestion or those whose memories seemed most garbled by the chronal shift. We chose times where society was equipped to accept them and avoided eras with minimal social adaptation measures. Others have been recruited.

«later»

I've been assigned to help one of the refugees; her name is Plestra Tuckr. Actually, I switched my lot to get her. This is the woman who ran from me during the evac. I'm glad to be able to help her at last.

2011 CE
Bohai Sea, China

Plestra and I are setting down in Japan to infiltrate a very well-organized ring of protesters; we're posing as international representatives of Greenpeace. Just days earlier, a massive oil spill occurred, covering a portion of the Bohai Sea ten times the size of ancient Chang'An. Riots and demonstrations broke out in Japan nearly immediately. Our tethers tell us that the massive public demonstrations and worldwide media attention on ConocoPhillips and the Chinese National Offshore Oil Company do not fit with this time.

«later»

The riots are causing deaths now. Huge sections of Kyoto have been burned, homes lost, businesses and ancient temples destroyed. A major organo-chemtech research facility has been gutted. Violence among the protesters is being encouraged in a decentralized way, and in response martial law is being discussed. Also, a major international crisis is brewing. Japanese public opinion is focusing the blame on China and the spill, and heated exchanges are crossing the Sea of Japan. There have been rumors of a mysterious opalescent submarine sighted in the ocean. Both the governments of China and Japan are blaming each other for its appearance, calling it a threat to their national security.

«later»

We've learned that an inner ring of organizers had published information about the spill before it happened. It must be a time hopper. Plestra has earned the trust of one of the inner circle. She's going to make a contact tomorrow and learn more.

«later»

Plestra came back from her meeting looking shaken. She said she'd met someone named Guntar Kasih, and that we needed to go to another time to head off the events in this frame. I sent the time coords in, and we're planning a jump. I can't get her to tell me more about what has affected her so deeply. I wonder if it was something that reminded her of the meteor strike. Perhaps we've put her in the field too soon?

2536 CE
Dronning Maud Land, Antarctica

Plestra's informant let her know that events in this time and place are about to tip a major shift that will not only start an ahistorical war between Japan and China in the 21st century but will also affect the development of the Abyssal Terran colonies, which become so important later on. We've dropped into the newly established Amundscott. It is the prime settlement on Antarctica, colonized after rising global temperatures make Antarctica one of the more habitable places for post-plague humans to live on the planet. We have cover identities from the Watch and are helping with the construction projects.

«later»

We've been here for two months now, and we've gotten to know the three-score colonists very well. The tether seems to be heating up, and we expect the Event to happen any time now. Plestra is so happy. She's befriended the pair of scientists heading the mission, Bulan Cahaya and Bima Kasih. I'm going to recommend that she be offered early detachment from the Watch to be placed in this time. Her trauma is going to take a long time to heal, and it would be better to have her do that here, where she can do so much good.

«later»

A kidnapper has taken the twins Darma and Guntar Kasih, the nine-year-old children of the two prominent Indonesian scientists Plestra has grown close to. Our tether tells us that these two are responsible for innovating the technology that makes Abyssal colonies possible in later centuries. Why didn't we get that intelligence earlier?

«later»

They're gone. We have Darma, but Guntar is gone. With Plestra. I can't believe it. She knew all along that the twins were the pivot here. She withheld communiqué from the tether from the rest of us. When we caught her on the cliffs with the twins, I was able to wrestle Darma away from her, but she held Guntar and dove into the ocean.

«later»

I've asked for extended leave. My briefing officer says she is going to recommend I receive it.

JOURNAL OF LIU FEIYAN.

3213 CE

I've been pulled from leave early. My briefing officer tells me it will be for the best. Talking about getting back on horses. They've sent me to the Ur-Tibetan plain to attend the peace talks between the Matriarchy's Abyssal Federation and the Joint Coordinated Terran Forces. My cover is to represent the Pan-Oceanic interests, and my tether tells me that something is very wrong.

«later»

The Tibetan shore is beautiful during the darkening twilight. We've all received the phenotypic gene therapy to better absorb the low oxygen in the atmosphere, and it affects us in different ways. I felt like there was a fish-eye lens on the world for the first few days. I thought I saw Plestra for a moment, but it was just an Abyssal delegate who looked a bit like her. I'm adapting now, and the effect is wearing off.

«later»

The signing is tonight. The Abyssals have requested that the signing happen in their transloc dome rather than on the mountain island as planned. My diplomatic team is handling the negotiations, but they seem to be intransigent on this point. I saw the woman who looked like Plestra again – no, this time I am sure. It is her.

«later»

We couldn't stop the change in location, and we're all to blame now. The dome has been crashed by an insane vision. A spiral pearl shell–and–steel subship is ramming the composite plates of the dome. I'm dumping protocol to make short hops with as many of the delegates as I can back up to the mountain. This one looks familiar to me.

«later»

I've subdued Guntar Kasih. He's been working with Plestra to undermine the peace. Apparently their first attempt was to try to end the development of the organo-chemtech which would be needed to make Abyssal colonies. He's raving about 21st-century devastation to the oceans, and how humans should have learned their lesson long before they lost the land. I've never met someone so anti-Abyssal, and anti-Epiterran at the same time. The boy looks to be about 33. Plestra must have used his genius to grow this nautilus ship that they attacked us with.

2582 CE

The first long-term research shelter should be being placed on the floor of the Bellingshausen Abyssal Plain, by Darma Kasih and her brother Guntar Kasih. Instead, I'm bringing him here, a prisoner, ten years older than his twin due to time asynchronization. I'm hoping that she can bring him back to some kind of reason. Her work in his absence has been even more focused on developing sub-oceanic dwelling arcologies. She went in a totally different direction from what I saw in 4507 CE though.

«later»

The twins remembered one another, even after all of this time. Darma was talking with Guntar when Plestra broke in, captaining the spiral submarine. She and her cohorts have boarded the shelter and are taking us all prisoner.

«later»

Guntar is dead. He pretended to rejoin Plestra, then shot her, disrupting the primitive shield they have on this seafloor shelter. I've commandeered the nautilus and have the surviving colonists, attackers, and Darma on board. Plestra is here as well, though she's been gravely wounded.

4508 CE

TimeWatch has given the go-ahead for us to change the transfer assessment for Plestra Tuckr. They maintain that the bilocation ban must be upheld, though, so we had to send the information via a fresh agent.

«later»

We've gotten her assent to resettle her on Antarctica in 2536 CE. Her skills will be needed, and this will snip the loop of her meeting Guntar and herself in 2011 which started us on all the other paths.

I can feel the paradox eating away at me, trying to sweep me out of the world. But you know what? It's worth it.

end

LIU FEIYAN.

JOURNAL OF LUCAS LEE.

LUCAS LEE.

1875 CE –

JOURNAL OF LUCAS LEE.

130 CE, JUNE 15
Rome, morning.

Nothing compares to watching someone fight for their life. Gladiator shows are the whole experience. Starting with fresh street food on the way, then walking by the foot of the three-story bronze Helios Colossus, standing outside the amphitheater. The crowd and heat inside is intense. The music barely audible over the roars. The buildup, seeing who's fighting today, knowing they must be thinking about whether today is their last day alive.

Going to a civilized sports match just doesn't compare, and I can't go anymore. This day, my Roman friends had good seats, Gate XI, but it was just an ordinary *munus*, not a special day. There's been so many time travelers watching the big celebratory games that TimeWatch restrict access. Otherwise, whole audience might turn out to be time travelers.

We'd just settled in, while the names of the criminals were being announced, and were deep in debate about where we would go for lunch, when a messenger boy pushed through to me with a tablet (wax, not computer). It was a message from the shift captain asking me back to base. Just as the executions of the criminals started. The whole of time to choose, and he chooses then.

The message said, in code of course, that there was a problem with 20th-cent Europe. I made my excuses, headed back to my *insula* (apartment) and jumped.

234,898 BCE

The first sign this mission wasn't going to be easy. My autochron had been tampered with. I appeared knee deep in a swampy forest, near two large spotted leopard-/tiger-looking beasts. PaciFist still worked fortunately. Checking, my autochron had been jammed to do only random time jumps, so I wasn't going to risk jumping with it again, unless I had no other option. There are stories of agents jumping using broken autochrons and then never existing. No thanks.

The tampering tells me I'm dealing with an enemy who knows about TimeWatch, knows I'm the agent getting the mission, and knows enough about an autochron's tech to break it. Not good. On the upside, however, a smarter opponent wouldn't randomize it, they'd send me to nowhen, and watch me to ensure I didn't escape.

I tried fixing it in the swamp, but couldn't. It was also getting dark – the tigery things were coming round. I didn't know when I was, but I had confidence that a future me will have known when I was, and would have put a spare autochron behind that tree, which I will have done. I mean there was one there. Time travel really mangles tenses.

I noted my time and place coords for future saving-my-hide action, and pinged a message upstream with the autochron to Prof. Juliet to meet me in Paris in 1919.

1919 CE, AUGUST 1
Paris.

Met the lovely professor at Café du Dôme, Montparnasse. She's an industrial-era expert and confused as well. Seems the Great War ended too early. France capitulated, and Britain and Russia sued for peace. No mass death in the trenches. Seemed like an improvement to me, but for that I got a lecture over bean stew on the European wars that were needed to set in motion the something or other. I'd missed lunch in Rome, but the menu was rather paltry – I expect better food in France. Maybe that was a side effect of losing the war. Juliet thought the divergence started in 1914, that the Germans kept sweeping across France and achieved the Schlieffen Plan. Start at the Battle of the Marne, it was lost instead of drawn, she said. So that's where I'm going. She wanted to stay in alternate Paris and study the impact. I arranged to meet her in 1918 when I've sorted it.

1914 CE, SEPTEMBER 8
Châtillon-sur-Seine.

At the French Army HQ, Marshall Joffre was there, the man in charge. The French front was already collapsing, and the British Expeditionary Force was hightailing it to the coast and safety. Joffre's driver is a maniac, but they're rushing around too late. I sneak into the HQ room when he's out and study the map. It looks like the French 6th Army has retreated in this timeline, allowing the Germans to advance on Paris. According to Cass, my tether, in the real timeline, Gallieni ordered the 6th Army to counterattack and reinforced them with hundreds of Paris taxis to transport 10,000 troops to shore them up.

1914 CE, SEPTEMBER 2
Paris.

I mingle in the chaotic Parisian HQ. Gallieni was old and tired, and not doing what he should. He's either been persuaded, controlled, or changed. He's human, but chem sensors pick up hypnagogic influencers on him – someone is altering his medication.

DNA analysis of his medical kit gets an odd result, chimp DNA. Freaky. Gallieni found me though, and I had to pretend to be a Deuxième Bureau agent. I tell him that one of his aides is a German spy, and I was investigating. He called them in, I tested each of them and found one was an uplifted chimp in a full-body disguise suit.

Under interrogation, Diego the chimp claimed to be part of a direct-action group for animal rights, called We Are People. He's here to stop the "slaughter of millions of horses" in the war. He clammed up then, but the suit was clearly 23rd-century tech. Cass knew nothing about WAP, but said uplifting started in 2212 in the Fontes Institute, with the first subjects getting their freedom in 2223.

I stick chronal interdiction handcuffs on him so he doesn't rescue himself. Gallieni was bursting with questions, so I stunned and MEM-tagged him.

Using the disguise suit I let Gallieni decide to defend Paris, and order the taxis to take troops to the front to reinforce the line.

1918 CE, AUGUST 1
Paris.

Met Prof. Juliet at the café, and confirmed I've restored the slaughter of WWI, both horses and men. Good job, she says.

TIMEWATCH CITADEL.

I drop Diego off at the Citadel prison and head on. Maybe they exile him to a prison parallel, maybe they recruit him, maybe they send him back to the distant past. I can't blame him, but you know, there are rules.

JULY 2223 CE, 2ND 16TH
São Paulo.

The Fontes Institute building was boarded up, but the Infocomm net tells me there were eight uplifts released to citizenship, including Diego. The institute experimented on them and others to enhance their intelligence, until the government decided that they'd gone far enough and they had rights like AIs did (the Gloaming

AI aside), and were owed a lot of damages. That, and fees from the entertainment news channels, made those eight rich.

Time travel was not commonly discovered at this time, so how did they do it? Intelligent chimps stand out even in 23rd-century Brazil, so I spend a week watching them. They met daily at an office rented under the name We Are People. Diego is still there, he's not gone back yet. One called Angelo seemed to be the leader. I wanted to get in to their meeting, but only chimps were invited, and they paid for strong e-privacy. I can't get their data and I can't listen in. So they're up to something, but what? Even the go-back-and-become-an-old-friend routine isn't going to work here, unless I want to be an uplifted chimp for ten years. And I don't do real-time.

Then one day eight turn up but only four leave the room. I checked, and the room was empty. Time to act.

One of them looked like a weaker link, Teodoro. I zap into his apartment that night and give him the Scary TimeCop routine, threatened to leave him with the dinosaurs or undo his uplift. He cracked easily and told me Angelo had several time devices coming for a mission to stop humans hurting animals. The uplifts were divided into teams of two, each tasked with one time period. His was persuading St. Augustine to write vegetarianism into Christianity. He doesn't know where Angelo got the devices, but he knew they were going to appear today. Teodoro tells me the devices just appeared on the table, and the active team members grabbed them and jumped. I need to find who sent them, otherwise, they'll just change time. I didn't notice at the time, but there was no meat on the Café du Dôme's menu, and meat in this time is purely vat grown. The world is vegetarian now, which ain't right.

Someone got a message to Angelo and the devices, but there's 11 years it could have happened in, and I ain't spending that long in real-time. But I had an idea.

130 CE, JUNE 10
Rome.

I hide and watch my own *insula* from across the road. One day the younger me leaves (for the baths, I think it was, that day), and a hooded stranger breaks in as soon as I've gone. He tampered with my autochron, and I stun him after he's done that. I have to let him still do it as it's in my time stream. Lying there he reverts to his natural form, a time-raptor. I cuff him, and we go back to the Citadel.

JOURNAL OF LUCAS LEE.

TIMEWATCH CITADEL.

He's called Trakkij and says he was just trying to save all the animals of the world from being hurt and killed by humans. I hand him over to the officer in charge of the Citadel prison and take a spare autochron from stores. They may trade him back to his clan, but I hope he learns his lesson. It's not like he's a vegetarian himself.

130 CE, JUNE 15
Rome, lunch.

I got back to my seat and friends in the amphitheater for the next games, the *venationes*, but watching panthers and lions getting killed had lost its appeal today, so I excused myself and jumped away. I will return to this day later, after I've had some time.

TIMEWATCH CITADEL.

Another day, another mission. The Citadel operates on a 24-hour clock for our sanity. My briefing officer asked me to investigate a cult that had caused an unexpected world war in the 2100s. Sometimes changes are subtle and take time to have an effect that the monitors notice. The war was obvious, but the divergence looked like it started a lot earlier.

The cult started gaining power in the mid-21st. Thierry, the social anthropologist on duty, scowled every time I called it a cult. Apparently the "neo-religion" existed in the normal timeline but didn't do a lot. It certainly didn't cause a worldwide schism and religious war. I'll start at the first obvious divergence point.

2056 CE, JULY 4
New York.

The city is covered in posters and adverts for Tildeonics, this new religion/cult. So many people are joining it's beginning to affect politics and media, and scaring the other, old, religions. TV anchors are talking about it. Cultists are donating huge sums of money.

I found and popped along to one of the intro/brainwashing classes. Apparently it's genuine cult stuff. They talked endlessly about how all of Tildeonics' founder's predictions have come true, and there's something else the cultists are really confident about, but only the highest acolytes know what that is. Their website gives their history. They were founded by a British self-publicist by the name Albert Tilden in the 1920s, and spread worldwide following his ascension. Their words.

They simply require all your money and time, and promise the usual everlasting life.

I don't like doing this normally, but I used a psy-reader on a senior cultist as she left the meeting. She'd seen the predictions Albert made, prophesying specific news events that had come perfectly true, and his notes on advanced quantum physics that scientists were only just catching up with now. Cheap tricks if you've got a time machine. But she was a fervent convert.

I needed to meet Albert, but he'd disappeared on his mystical comet in 1930. At least, that's what the literature says.

1928 CE, FEBRUARY 3
London.

A meeting about Tildeonics in a draughty hall, with Albert himself. He talked movingly about the gifts he had received from the spirit guardians and that he will be taken up to a wandering star and restored to Earth when it returns. He'd written it all down in his books of prophesy, 2s each, or £1 the set. He was a natural presenter and held the audience's attention. I quizzed the people sat near me about him. He had become famous in 1911 with his "Disappearing Bull" trick. According to Cass, my tether, the Disappearing Donkey should be done first by Morritt in 1912, and then Houdini did his Disappearing Elephant in 1918. Albert's stolen their magic. Making large animals vanish was peak popular entertainment at the time. I hung around and managed to get a quick chat with Albert before he left. He seemed keen for me to join, with a donation, of course. Time to visit the theater.

1911 CE, DECEMBER 11
London.

There are posters everywhere advertizing "Tilden's Disappearing Bull!" part of *Maskelyne and Devant's Mysteries* show at the St. George's Hall theater 7:30 p.m. every night this week. Also All Sold Out. I pretended to be an American impresario and went to the hall early. I met Devant, a magician who ran the theater, and got an invite to the show that night.

When I got there the place was already heaving. The show was good fun with six or seven acts. At the end a young Albert did his Disappearing Bull trick spectacularly. He built up the tension, and after 20 minutes of showmanship, the bull was led into a wooden box suspended off the ground. Albert whipped the crowd up, and the sides of the box collapsed – no bull to be seen. The crowd went wild. Devant leaned to me, "I have no idea how he does it, but he's making a lot of money."

I have an idea of how he's doing it, and I doubt it's magic.

I break into his rooms at the theater that night. His trunk was padlocked, but opened easily. Inside, I found an American news magazine from Jun 2055 and a tablet computer, but no time device. I know what he's doing now, I just need to find the other end.

2055 CE, JUNE 29
New York.

With the serial number of the tablet, Cass hacked the manufacturers online warranty database and got me the name of the purchaser. A Dr. Bree Wilks, Stanford University. She's a quantum-field PhD student, and well regarded. Too early for time travel.

2055 CE, JUNE 29
Stanford.

Dr. Wilks was a cool customer. I turned up at her lab, and I could see there was damage to walls and equipment. She was smart, and in the end I came clean about who I was, and asked whether she'd seen anything strange. She relaxed and told me her story. She'd been experimenting with quantum-field experiments, in her own time, when one morning there was a goat in the lab. She managed to get rid of it out of a window, but another appeared a few days later, then a bull, then three bulls. In the end she paid a local butcher to come and collect them. She had accidentally generated a time-hole with her experiment, and she was trying to work out what had happened when I arrived. The equipment was still on, humming in the center of the room. It looked quite simple, but I'm a user not a designer.

She'd never heard of Albert Tilden, but she confirmed her tablet had been stolen. There had also been small, bare footprints in the room.

JOURNAL OF LUCAS LEE.

She was too smart and too curious to leave with this knowledge and equipment, so I pinged TimeWatch HR instead of MEM-tagging her. She'd fit in well with us.

Which left Albert. I could switch Bree's machine off, but then he wouldn't disappear in 1930, as he hadn't arrived here yet. I could take the equipment to a wandering star and watch him fulfill his prophecy, but Cass reminded me he hadn't killed anyone or abused time, except accidentally. In the end it was easiest to wait for him to come through, stun him and drag him off to the Citadel. Two more bulls for the butcher. Then I smashed the device and took Bree's notes.

TIMEWATCH CITADEL.

I recommend all new agents visit the Citadel prison, Eternity some call it, at least once. Certain criminals need to be kept out of time, or have escaped prison dimensions too often. The names of those kept are secret to protect against paradoxes; apparently an agent saw his own name on there once. It's heavily guarded for sure. A reliable source on the inside told me that cell J7 is the Fungus Cell, a prisoner mind controlled by a Colony outbreak. I guess they are keeping it alive to get at its cross-time knowledge, perhaps?

Got a message from my briefing officer. A TimeWatch researcher has started stunning civilians in 1978, and clearly he needs assistance. That means either a new recruit got themselves into a time loop mess or someone's gone rogue. The researcher is Bennell, according to the records I'm allowed to retrieve. I know him a little, always seemed a little jumpy. His last mission was to investigate a singularity event that had been stopped in 2138. Cass, my tether, tells me that means a non-Gloaming AI nearly achieved runaway sentience, grabbing power and systems before it was shut down. If it was nearly as bad as the Gloaming Incident, that's something that we don't even joke about anymore.

1978 CE, MAY 10
New York.

I get into a paramedic outfit from the Citadel wardrobe department, and jump to a deserted alley near where Bennell will start shooting. I could see him, standing in the crowd shouting, "It's all wrong!" like a madman; the passersby have obviously seen this before and ignore him.

I've brought a stretcher with me and hide my autochron in it. It's set to auto-follow if he jumps. As I approach him, he recognizes me and draws his PaciFist, but I'm ready and he goes down. Oddly, everyone just walks around his body. I strap him to the stretcher, but something is wrong. Two policemen stroll by and don't even ask what's happening. It's New York in the '70s, but still.

He's got money in his pocket, so I wheel him into the alley and buy a local newspaper from a kiosk. Cass scans it and confirms everything looks OK – the timeline corresponds exactly to her records of the news. I check; Bennell's autochron was last used two days ago, from 2138. I take his tether, which called itself AX42.

I handcuff him to the stretcher and slap a MEM-tag on him, with instructions to keep him sedated until I return. My plan is to hop a short way forward, just to check everything is alright.

1979 CE, MAY 10
New York.

It can be hard to tell sometimes if something has changed. If a war doesn't start or the wrong president is elected it's easy, but subtle changes can have big effects downstream that are really hard to pinpoint. You need tools to detect them without having to check everyone on the planet to see if they do what they should have done. I often use stock market numbers. They're easy to get and combine a lot of different social, financial, and political effects into one measure. It can start to tell me what's changed, where or when to start looking. Oil price higher than it should be? Share price of airlines down? Small changes don't have long lasting effects on the timeline though, the numbers return back to the normal values quickly.

One year on, I step out of the alley again and buy another *New York Times* from the same kiosk. The NYSE Composite was exactly what the timeline record showed it should be today. Every number I checked was right. I should go back to the Citadel. Instead, I decide to track Bennell's movements. If he went berserk, there was probably a good reason.

2138 CE, DECEMBER 3
Hyderabad.

I jump in just before Bennell arrives at the start of his mission. I follow him to the office of Rosana-Ima, Head of EI Research (emergent intelligence apparently – Cass said "artificial intelligence" was felt by some to be derogatory). Cass also hacked an external cleaning drone so we could listen in to Bennell's conversation.

JOURNAL OF LUCAS LEE.

He was pretending to be a government regulator and Rosana-Ima was explaining what happened. On the evening of 21st November, their EI, ERIN, had gained more intelligence than they realized and set off on a virtuous spiral. As it got smarter, it used resources better and could find ways to access more resources and make itself smarter again. It took over other research computers and labs until fail-safes shut it down after 141 minutes. She gave him all the logs.

I'd gone cold. Civilians don't remember the Gloaming Incident, but the virtuous spiral was far from virtuous. We're lucky anyone survived. I don't want it to happen again.

I asked AX42, and it showed us all the logs they'd been given. We spent an hour trying to find clues from the data before realizing these logs were faked. I argued with damn AX42; it finally told us that Bennell had thought the same and had hidden a monitoring device the day before the event that showed there was a time fluctuation 15 seconds before the EI was shut down. My guess is that it sent its intelligence to somewhere else, knowing it was about to get switched off. Bennell had jumped to 1978, but I wanted to see the event.

2138 CE, NOVEMBER 21
Hyderabad.

Using Cass I tracked the event online. ERIN took over a satellite dish and sent a cry for help out into space while it tried to find a way to overcome the fail-safes. Seventy-nine minutes later it had a response from space, a large data packet from Jupiter's direction. ERIN immediately built a device and sent a self-replicating factory back in time. The logs had been totally faked. If it's Jupiter, I'm guessing Europans; they don't normally go in for technology, but they surely do hate humanity. Rosana-Ima must be controlled.

2138 CE, DECEMBER 4
Hyderabad.

I stunned Rosana-Ima, checked her tongue, and found the Europan parasite staring back at me. Then everyone started attacking me, hundreds of people, controlled. Stunned many and only just got away by emergency jump.

JOURNAL OF LUCAS LEE.

1979 CE, MAY 10
New York, p. m.

There was a message written on the wall. "Time agent, I have done what you want to do. Every human from 1978 onwards does exactly what the timeline record says they did. They have no choice, I control their decisions. The timeline cannot alter now. Go home. ERIN".

Well, crap.

Outside the alley it was like being in a 3-D film – everyone acted normally but ignored me. Nothing I did changed what ERIN had told them to do that day. They were people without free will, living their life, but not living it. In space, or hidden around the world, ERIN's nanobot factories were converting people into flesh robots.

2138 CE, NOVEMBER 21
Hyderabad.

I connected Cass to the satellite dish. I didn't want to stop the event, nor the 1978 time jump; I'd seen it, Bennell had seen it, and paradox would be painful. So when the Europans' data packet arrived back, Cass intercepted it and tweaked the contents. The time fluctuation happened as I'd seen, but the beamed-out nanobot factory ended up in the heart of the sun.

I stuck around long enough to have a drink. I felt I deserved it.

TIMEWATCH CITADEL.

It took a long time to convince Bennell that everything was back to normal. HQ is following up ERIN's communication with Europa. And I'm heading to Tortuga for another drink.

1642 CE, AUGUST 29
Tortuga.

Terrible day. I spent the night drinking and partying with the Brethren of the Coast around town. This morning they were scattered, mostly sleeping or off in rooms with partners. I was considering returning to the Citadel when I appeared at the tavern door, bleeding. It was me, but an older, later me, in a battered TimeWatch uniform. I was bleeding. He, me, shouted my name, "Lucas!" The other me was perhaps ten years older? We age differently, so could be more. I felt the universe tearing with paradox. He looked at me and said, I think, "The other TimeWatch!" as he was blasted in the back by a beam cannon.

Yeah, it's going to be a terrible day.

end

JOURNAL OF KATIA FILIPOVNA AND TEAM.

KATIA FILIPOVNA.

1902 CE –

JOURNAL OF KATIA FILIPOVNA AND TEAM.

1922, DECEMBER 1: KATIA FILIPOVNA.
New York City.

While our team was investigating historical forgeries, we noticed unfamiliar "snakes in a sarcophagus" novelty items among other pieces of Egyptomania in a New York store. Shopkeeper explained that these had become a best-selling item after the unexplained incident at Tut's tomb.

«later»

Researched discovery of Tutankhamun's tomb in New York Public Library newspaper collection. Accounts confirm that, upon opening the tomb, Howard Carter was deluged by modern prank snakes, the kind that had been sold in a can. Cartoons depict a Carter covered in snakes; Carter and Lord Carnarvon attempting to revive Carnarvon's daughter, Evelyn; and artists' concepts of ancient Egyptians performing such jokes. Several weeks afterward, major newspapers feature ads for Snakes in a Sarcophagus: "Make your friends scream for their MUMMY!"

1322 BCE: KATIA FILIPOVNA.
Valley of the Tombs, Egypt.

Given the complexity of traveling into a sealed tomb from above, we chose to enter the tomb disguised as a team of painters. Once we found an isolated location within the tomb, we jumped to the night before its unsealing.

1922 CE, NOVEMBER 25: KATIA FILIPOVNA.
Valley of the Tombs, Egypt.

Snakes present in tomb morning before the discovery. Initiating search for the culprit using binary time search method.

1922 CE, NOVEMBER 12: KATIA FILIPOVNA.
Valley of the Tombs, Egypt.

Concluded binary time jump search. After determining snakes in evidence the morning of November 13 but not the 11th, arrived morning of the 12th to camp out and wait. Fatima got some excellent recordings of the hieroglyphs to augment the footage at HQ.

«later»

Apprehended Keisha Harris, traveling from 2748. Harris explained that she planned to record the incident for a PRANX holo competition. In preparation for the launch of its products, PRANX, Inc. has offered a prize for the best classic prank in a historical period. The winner receives 40,000 credits, and the holo will be used in PRANX marketing with credit. Harris hoped the exposure would land her an advertising contract. We advised Harris of the ill advisedness of her plan and are returning with her to 2748.

1922 CE, NOVEMBER 26: KATIA FILIPOVNA.
PRANX holo contest entry for Keisha Harris.
Subject: Tut's tomb.

(00:00:00) [from a device planted inside the tomb] The video begins in utter darkness as a scraping sound is heard. (00:00:30) Cracks of dusty light outline the door as it is wrested open. (00:01:14) The door opens wide enough to admit Howard Carter's head. Its motion triggers an enormous can of spring-loaded prank snakes which send Carter backward, screaming in terror. (00:01:32) [recording switches to an exterior holo-shot] Carter and Carnarvon attempt to revive the latter's daughter, Evelyn, who has fainted from the shock. (00:01:41) Carter's face is livid as he shouts curses before returning to gather up the snakes.

2748 CE: KATIA FILIPOVNA.
London, England.

Harris showed us the message she received. Hacking reveals it was sent through an anonymous holo network to an unknown number of persons. Turns out Harris is a minor holo-celebrity with a channel dedicated to offbeat historical incidents. Her TimeWatch record reveals she is a known player but her recordings had never interfered with the timeline and thus she had not been subjected to monitoring. Upgrading her status to the TimeWatch watch list, advised her to keep this secret, and will take no further action here.

JOURNAL OF KATIA FILIPOVNA AND TEAM.

«later»

Unable to track PRANX, Inc. any further in the holo network. Worked with HQ to find other amusing historical incidents which resemble classic pranks. Was given a list of four possibilities to track down. Extracting data from the messages each of these people received should give us sufficient data, combined with Mandy 9000's talents in 23rd-century hacking, to locate the original sender. The team has decided to split up and each take one of the four problem spots. Fatima will head back here in London (1800), Mandy 9000 expressed interest over a linguistic concern in *The Travels of Marco Polo* (1301), Jun will take Alexander Graham Bell (1876), and I propose to handle a tricky issue concerning Ulysses S. Grant (1865).

1800 CE, MAY 15: FATIMA (KATIA FILIPOVNA'S TEAM).
London, England

London is abuzz with the story of how, when the king entered his box at Theatre Royal in Drury Lane, a man stood up and pretended to shoot him. Rather than a bullet, however, his pistol produced a small flag with the King's Colors and the word BANG! embroidered across it. My tether indicates that this must be James Hadfield, who failed to assassinate King George III.

«later»

A brief interview with Hadfield convinces me he thought the gun genuine and had tested it. Ascertained the times he slept last night.

1800 CE, MAY 14: FATIMA (KATIA FILIPOVNA'S TEAM).
Residence of James Hadfield in London.

Entered Hadfield's room while he slept. Found working pistol. I plan to remain until he shows signs of awakening before leaving. I must find out when the pistol was swapped.

«later»

Apprehended Manjeet Gabir in Hadfield's quarters around 5 a.m. Escorted him elsewhere to talk. Gun in his possession had the "BANG!" flag, and when I confiscated it he protested that fabricating a duplicate and creating a believable flag had cost him considerable time and money. Gabir is a graduate student at the New Delhi Institute of Political Science and writing a thesis on Indo-British relations in the 18th century. He was unsure why he received the message, although he subscribes to several dozen holo channels. Obtained Gabir's copy of the message and transmitted data log to Mandy 9000.

1800 CE, MAY 15: KATIA FILIPOVNA.
PRANX holo contest entry for Manjeet Gabir. Subject: James Hadfield.

(00:00:00) The orchestra finishes tuning their instruments before launching into "God Save the King." (00:00:20) [angle shifts to view from box opposite the royal box] King George enters from the back and takes four steps forward before pausing, eyes fixed on something in the audience. (00:00:27) [angle from a recording device just below the king's box] A man in the front right of the audience, James Hadfield, has stood and points a pistol at the king. He fires. A loud bang causes the audience to scream, but instead of a bullet, a British flag with the word BANG! embroidered on it pops out. The device zooms in on Hadfield's confused face as he begins to shake with tears. Royal guards rush in and arrest him.

1301 CE: MANDY 9000 (KATIA FILIPOVNA'S TEAM).
Pisa, Italy.

Met at a tavern with Rustichello da Pisa concerning his authorship of *Livre des Merveilles du Monde,* more commonly known now as *The Travels of Marco Polo.* Questioned him particularly about the account of his discovery of the small city of "Culu-stan." The author seems aware of the unlikeliness of finding a region whose name translates to "buttocks-land," particularly as humans consider these enlarged muscle-fiber bundles designed to aid in bipedal locomotion to be hilarious. Yet he insists that Polo seemed as sincere and befuddled by the incident as he did. He does not appear to be lying.

1271 CE: MANDY 9000 (KATIA FILIPOVNA'S TEAM).
80.34 km west of Kashgar along the silk road.

Apprehended group of time travelers with the supplies to build a "Potemkin village" in Polo's path. These men and women belong to a Chinese sketch comedy team, the "Hu Crew." One of their signature gag series involves incidents in which they pretended to meet Marco Polo and give him false information for humorous purposes. This particular sketch involved a village whose language coincidentally had many Latin vulgarities as common words. For example, they called all food "merda." My co-workers may appreciate this. Dispersed group with a warning and confiscated a copy of the message they received. Will await reports from my teammates, then designate a meeting time and place near PRANX, Inc.'s headquarters.

1271 CE: KATIA FILIPOVNA.
PRANX holo contest entry for the Hu Crew. Subject: Marco Polo.

(00:00:00) An elaborate montage involving multiple time travelers building a Potemkin village in an empty region along the Silk Road. (00:01:03) One of the men, now dressed in a fur hat and embroidered robes, gives a thumbs-up sign to the recorder as a caravan of travelers pulls up. (00:01:20) Speaking Latin, a man comes forward and welcomes travelers to his town of Culu-stan.

1876 CE, MARCH 10: JUN KIM (KATIA FILIPOVNA'S TEAM).
Boston, Massachusetts.

An incident in the career of Alexander Graham Bell had led him to experiment with devices which he hoped could communicate with the spirit world. Given the nature of the pranks our team has encountered, I surmised that it would likely involve his invention of the telephone. My listening device detected a radio transmission interrupting that famous call to Watson and asking Bell if he had Prince Albert in a can. Bell seemed greatly shaken and asked if he was speaking to Prince Albert. Locked a signal on the location.

1876 CE, MARCH 10, EARLIER IN THE DAY: JUN KIM (KATIA FILIPOVNA'S TEAM).
Boston, Massachusetts.

Traveled to the early morning and installed a small radio blackout device enclosing Bell's laboratory. Spent much of the morning waiting near the location of the radio transmission. Apprehended three teenage Scots brothers – Brodie, Gavin, and Quinn Reid. Obtained Gavin's copy of the message and whisked them back to

JOURNAL OF KATIA FILIPOVNA AND TEAM.

Scotland 2748 CE for a word with their mother.

1876 CE, MARCH 10: JUN KIM (KATIA FILIPOVNA'S TEAM).
PRANX holo contest entry for Brodie, Gavin, and Quinn Reid.
Subject: Alexander Graham Bell.

(00:00:00) A handsome young man with a receding hairline and full black whiskers leans in to a conical device. "Mr. Watson," he begins. Suddenly, with a rush of background static, a voice erupts from the line. "Mr. Bell? [buzz] Hello, is this Alexander [buzz] Graham Bell?" The man starts backward. After a moment, he leans in again. "Yes, this is he. To whom am I speaking? How did you accomplish this?"

"Mr. Bell, do you have Prince Albert in a can?" asks the voice. Bell stares, befuddled. "Because you'd better let him out!" The raucous laughter of at least three persons causes tremendous static on the line, which then goes dead.

After a moment, a shaky voice buzzes through the device. "Bell? This is Watson. Who was that?"

Bell replies, "Mr. Watson – Come here – I want to see you."

1865 CE, APRIL 12: KATIA FILIPOVNA.
Appomattox, VA.

I took Ulysses S. Grant in part because his change seemed the hardest to track as it appeared to be the fear of a prank. Minor changes in biographies noted that he often sat himself awkwardly, gently lowering his body while feeling the cushion beneath him. The tendency became most pronounced during his presidency. It took multiple jumps, but I managed to speak with his aide-de-camp Brevet Brigadier General Orville E. Babcock during the celebration of Lee's surrender.

After several drinks, I asked Babcock whether Grant had been nervous about anything going wrong during the surrender. Babcock laughed and told me that the general's greatest fear was of someone placing a strange device on his chair before he sat down. This device would emulate a loud flatulent noise. The general had sat on them during his first class at West Point, at his wedding breakfast, and while speaking with President Lincoln just a year ago. He'd asked Babcock to watch the chair any time he stood.

JOURNAL OF KATIA FILIPOVNA AND TEAM.

1839 CE, SEPTEMBER: KATIA FILIPOVNA.
West Point, NY.

On a hunch, I traveled first to the time of the West Point incident. Though the travelers did a decent job of being unobtrusive, I was able to single them out as they made their way toward Grant's classroom. I quietly identified myself as an agent of TimeWatch and asked them to come quietly with me. The pair was a middle-aged Tennessee couple, Janet and Veronica Foster, American First Civil War buffs.

Veronica Foster's nephew had been the one to receive the message, and the pair had a long-standing preference for the strategies of Union general George Henry Thomas. While they did not wish to do something so serious as alter the course of the war, they thought it a funny gag to play on the man who ended up with glory they rightfully considered Thomas'. Both agreed to drop the plan and seemed mildly embarrassed.

2748 CE: KATIA FILIPOVNA.
Crabtree, TN.

Spoke with Veronica Foster's nephew and retrieved his copy of the message for Mandy 9000.

1839–1865: KATIA FILIPOVNA.
PRANX holo contest entry for Janet and Veronica Foster.
Subject: Ulysses S. Grant.

(00:00:00) A West Point classroom full of 17-year-old boys stands as the teacher enters. They sit in unison, at which point the sound of flatulence interrupts their attempts at calm demeanor. A short student jumps up and stares in horror at his chair, while his classmates laugh. (00:00:52) The newlywed Ulysses S. and Julia Grant greet guests at their wedding breakfast. When Grant sits down, the same sound is heard again. A look of dawning horror creeps over Grant's face. (00:02:02) Grant, Secretary Stanton, and Lincoln enter a small drawing room in the White House. Lincoln gestures for Grant to take a seat. The tired Grant plops down on a sofa, which emits a flatulent sound. A furious Grant stands and throws a small cushion across the room. He kicks the leg of the sofa. (00:03:18) Before sitting down to await Lee's surrender, Grant bends over and searches his chair carefully. One hand remains on the seat cushion as he carefully lowers himself down. No sound occurs.

JOURNAL OF KATIA FILIPOVNA AND TEAM.

2748 CE: KATIA FILIPOVNA.
San Diego, CA.

Mandy 9000 broke into the PRANX HQ two nights before the transmission was sent and booked us an appointment the next day. They're located in what apparently used to be a beauty salon, not far outside San Diego. The next morning we met with PRANX's advertising manager, who doubles as their technology officer. He attempted to bluff his way past our assertions but eventually admitted to the plan. Unfortunately, he proved adamant about the strategy. The company's entire focus is retro pranks and this advertising strategy has been a part of the company since its conception two years ago. We did get information about the circumstances of the company's founding.

Mandy 9000 wrote a program which will send the message in two days, tracing information and all, but only to the five groups of people to whom we have spoken.

2746 CE: KATIA FILIPOVNA.
San Diego, CA.

MEM-tagged PRANX founders after their initial meeting. TimeWatch HQ has devised an alternative advertising concept for them to work with and will implant that, while subtly adding suggestions against time travel.

On a related note, I sat on a whoopee cushion this morning and nobody on the team will tell me who's to blame.

end

THE HU CREW PREPARING FOR MARCO POLO.

Still from video. The Crew had no experience of working with large animals, so used replica horses that stand like the statues they are for the duration of the video.

KATIA FILIPOVNA.

KATIA FILIPOVNA.

JOURNALS OF RICHARD PLANTAGENET AND THOMAS WU.

RICHARD, DUKE OF YORK.

H.S S
RELIQUIÆ
EDWARDI V^{TI} REGIS ANGLIÆ ET RICHARDI DUCIS
EBORACENSIS
HOS, FRATRES GERMANOS, TURRE LONDIN.^{SI} CONCLUSOS
INIECTISQ CULCITRIS SUFFOCATOS,
ABDITE ET INHONESTE TUMULARI IUSSIT
PATRUUS RICHARDUS PERFIDUS REGNI PRÆDO
OSSA DESIDERATORUM, DIV ET MULTUM QUÆSITA,
POST ANNOS CXC&1A
SCALARUM IN RUDERIBUS (SCALA ISTÆ AD SACELLUM
TURRIS ALBÆ NUPER DUCEBANT)
ALTE DEFOSSA, INDICTIS CERTISSIMIS SUNT REPERTA
XVII DIE IULII A.O D.NI MDCLXXIIII
CAROLUS II REX CLEMENTISSIMU SACERBAM SORTEM MISERATUS
INTER AVITA MONUMENA PRINCIPIBUS INFELICISSIMIS.
IUSTA PERSOLVIT.
ANNO DOM.I 1678 ANNOQ REGNI SUI 30

3600 CE: THOMAS WU.
TimeWatch headquarters.

Just had to issue yet another reprimand to Kate Symond. Only she would think to rescue the Princes in the Tower.

Completely shameless about it, too. Faced me down in the infirmary as though I were the unreasonable one, with three-quarters of the medical staff watching. "What? I haven't changed a damned thing. They're not supposed to be there to affect history, and they're not there to affect history. The thug with the pillow thought he killed them, and the thug with the pillow still thinks he killed them. The bodies were never found; the bodies never will be found."

"And I can't have them sent back now, even if I wanted to," I said. I could feel a headache coming on. "Not without risking all kinds of paradox problems."

Symond did a reasonable impression of a woman who hadn't thought of that, not that I was fooled for a minute. "Huh," she said, and smiled at me. "Guess not."

And... she's right, I can't. She planned this one very well indeed.

So I brought the kids to live with the others in the TimeWatch orphanage, and then I went back to my office and put my most headache-inducing agent on restricted duty for six weeks.

The director keeps asking why I put up with this from her, but the fact is that Symond's just that good. Her results are so consistently spectacular that I'd put up with worse shenanigans than a predilection for rescuing children. Agents from collapsed timelines tend to have obsessive fixations; this is a completely understandable one.

3600 CE: THOMAS WU.
TimeWatch headquarters.

Yet another outburst over at the orphanage school today. Once again, with Richard Plantagenet behind it. To my astonishment and displeasure, Brigit called me. I asked why in the world she thought this was any of my business, and she explained that Kate Symond was away on assignment. When I didn't say anything, she added that, well, I was Kate's superior officer. Which I suppose she thought made me Richard's grand-whatever-it-is-Symond-is-to-Richard. Grand-adult–role model? The director has asked me more than once if it is really such a good idea for Symond to be modeling behavior to anyone, and it's becoming increasingly difficult to answer. We've had more schoolyard fights in the five years Richard has been with us than the fifteen years before that.

Talked with Edward about it later; the poor kid was brick red the whole time. It can't be easy for him to be saddled with a younger brother like Richard. It's all very well to excuse Richard's behavior by saying "childhood trauma," but Edward had exactly the same trauma, and look at him. The most promising of this year's trainees. It's a shame.

3609 CE: RICHARD PLANTAGENET.
TimeWatch headquarters.

Four a.m. I had that dream again. Not of the night in the Garden Tower, not of footsteps and creaking doors and down pillows – I don't dream of that. Not often, at least. I dream of church bells on a summer night, and the creaking of the postern gate as my mother opened it to hand me to my uncle's men.

We were in sanctuary. He had Edward, but we were safe. She stayed in sanctuary with my sisters for the rest of that year. But she gave me to him.

Two weeks later my brother and I were declared illegitimate, and four weeks later we were dead.

Nothing in the history books can tell me why she did it. Or why she came out of sanctuary herself the following year when she knew my uncle had ordered us killed. Or why she threw her support behind Henry Tudor in 1483 only to rejoin Uncle Richard's court mere months later.

Early historians say she was a flighty woman. She wasn't – that was the last thing she was; I remember that much about her. Later historians say she was ambitious. But that makes no sense; even if I was nothing more to her than a playing piece, how could relinquishing control of me possibly strengthen her position?

There must have been some other reason. I need to know how she could have given me away.

«later»

No. What I really need to do is fix the problem.

I have a bloody time machine.

Well, access to one, at least, even if I'm only in my first year of training.

And Kate says the person who sees a problem should fix the problem. That sometimes it is not only permissible but essential to take matters into one's own hands.

I can fix this. I know where the royal progress will take King Richard III after his coronation. A bullet through his head, and Edward gets his throne back, right? And then we'll have the lives we should have had; then there will be no need to fight back dreams of footsteps on the stairs of the Garden Tower. I can fix this for both of us.

1483 CE: RICHARD PLANTAGENET.

I wasn't expecting this.

I was expecting the autochron controls to misfire. I was expecting TimeWatch to be there to stop me. I was expecting the gun to jam. I was expecting the past to fight back as I tried to change it.

I wasn't expecting that it would work … and that Uncle Richard's death would change nothing.

Even with Richard III's brains splattered all over the forest floor, the Little Princes still died in the tower in the summer of 1483.

Is it possible Uncle Richard didn't order our deaths?

I have to think about this.

«later»

Empirical testing is the only way to know for sure. I reset the timeline so I can figure out what really happened without external influence. To do that, I had to stop myself from killing my uncle. The risk of paradox didn't really bother me (and doesn't seem to have had any negative lasting impact) but I was really hard to convince. (I'm never going to tell Edward this, but he might have a point. I really am kind of an asshole.)

So all is as it was. I'll slip in and out of the restored timeline until I understand where those orders came from. I can foil the plot later – next time through, even; what's life without a little paradox risk? – but first I need to understand what I am foiling.

Did she know? Is that why she let them take me? Did she know we had nothing to fear from my uncle, that the real enemy was someone else?

1486 CE: RICHARD PLANTAGENET.

I think I mis-set the controls because my hands were shaking so hard. By the time I realized I was in 1486, it was too late to go earlier without risking another paradox, and they're piling up around me with every step. I can feel time trying to sweep me away. And I didn't want to go back and muck with coordinates again; I needed to confront her right there and then. How could she have allowed my sister to marry that man? Did she buy her own safety by giving him Elizabeth?

There's something to be said for a simpler time; people might gasp at the sight of a ghost, but at least they don't run to phone the authorities, so you have a few minutes to explain yourself. The idea of time travel was obviously foreign to her, but it wasn't too difficult to communicate the basic principles. And I didn't have to spend any time convincing her of my identity.

"That's not the point," I said, when it seemed as though the conversation would founder on technicalities. "It doesn't matter where I've been. It matters that I was rescued. From assassins who came to the Garden Tower. Do you know who sent them?"

"I do," she said, watching me with confusion. "I thought it was your uncle Richard at first. That was why I gave Henry Tudor my support the first time he tried to take the crown, during Buckingham's rebellion. But when the rebellion was crushed, Richard proved to me that he had not given the order. He took your freedom and your brother's crown, but he never intended to take your lives. When I understood your blood was on Buckingham's hands, I reconciled with Richard, and wrote to your half brother the marquess to abandon support of Tudor. When I came out of sanctuary with your sisters, your uncle Richard treated us well."

"And when Tudor succeeded in taking Richard's crown, you reconciled with Tudor. How could you?"

She seemed even more confused. "Why would I not? Your uncle was dead; his supplanter offered to make my daughter his queen. Why should I not accept so fair a bargain?"

"Wait," I said. The thudding in my ears started to ease. "Do you not know? Haven't you realized who Buckingham did it for?"

She hadn't. I showed her the evidence I had collected, the trail that led from the assassin, to Buckingham, to the man who wed my sister to legitimize the throne he stole from the House of York.

The color drained from my mother's face, and she fumbled for the back of a chair. She managed to sit before her knees gave way, but it was a near thing.

The hell of it is, I'm not sure what we can do now. Even if I went back and slew Tudor as well as Buckingham, and slew Uncle Richard again before he could push through *Titulus Regius*, it might not fix the problem. Someone else might challenge Edward's claim. Someone else might take a pretender's coin and arrange for the assassination of the boy king. I don't think I can eliminate all the variables before the paradoxes smother me.

And we can't retake the throne now, in 1486. Edward's grown. I'm grown. The Little Princes are gone, even if they didn't die.

But letting Tudor keep my sister and my family's crown – No. We have to do something.

«later»

We've spent most of the last several nights talking. My mother is a shrewd woman with a strategist's mind. Flighty, my ass. History books are written by idiots.

We have a plan. It's too late for me to claim my own identity – a man of eighteen can't pass for a boy of twelve. But we could find a lad who looks like me. I could tutor him in how to behave, and then when the throne is his, I could stand behind it. And that would be just as good as sitting on it. My mother says so, at least, and she would know.

She thinks it would be best for me to pass myself off as a priest. Priests have the right kind of education – I could claim Oxford – and are granted more leniency. It will be easier for me to get where I need to go, and less likely I'll be summarily executed if this should all go wrong.

1487 CE: "FATHER RICHARD SYMOND" (FORMERLY RICHARD PLANTAGENET).

We're ready. Lambert and I leave for Ireland in the morning.

I went to see her one last time to tell her it was about to begin. I thought perhaps she would be startled when she came into her apartments to find me there, but she only smiled. "And people said *I* was a witch."

I finally asked her. It's the question that started all of this, the first falling domino. I understand why she came out of sanctuary after Edward's and my "death." I understand why she trusted Uncle Richard with her life and her daughters' lives though everyone thought he'd killed her sons.

But she didn't know any of that the night Richard's men came to take me from sanctuary. Yet she handed me over. And I still don't know why.

When I asked, her cheeks flushed. "I want you to know I have regretted that decision every day since the 22nd of June 1483. I don't know how to say this to you, but – my waiting woman convinced me you would be in no danger. It's not as mad as it sounds," she added hastily. "Lady Katherine had been with me many years, and she had the Sight. She'd foretold often what would happen, and what she said would come true always did. She said you would be safe. And I ... believed her."

Lady Katherine? "Did she by any chance disappear shortly after that night?" My mother nodded. "What did she look like?"

It seems she looked like Kate Symond. Only much older.

So ... it must be that this rebellion will work. It must be that I'll restore the throne to the House of York, and the only way I can be here to do so is if Kate rescues me from the Garden Tower. So I have to be in the Garden Tower to be rescued. So she took steps to ensure I would be.

So it's all right. It's all going to be all right.

1488 CE: EDWARD PLANTAGENET

[accidental tether recording]

"Get in the autochron."

[sound of book falling to floor] *"Edward?* How did you get in here? Are those ... Those are monk's robes." [deep breath, change in tone] "It's no surprise you've decided you have a vocation, big brother, but you do realize you could have picked a more comfortable century to –"

"Dressing as a priest was the only way I could convince them to let me inside the prison. I had to see where you were kept, so I turned up tomorrow and said I was here to shrive you."

"So that makes you ... Edward the Confessor?"

"That would be a more amusing jest if I were not imperiling my chronal stability, my career, and the bloody space-time continuum to clean up your mess. Get in the autochron."

"Wait. You're here to take me back? Not to help?"

[overlapping] "Help?"

[overlapping, speaking fast] "We're both here now. With a working time machine. We could try again. We could try earlier. Or later! We could come out of hiding in 1493, we'd be the right ages, it wouldn't even be a lie to say we are who we are, we could – This is supposed to be your throne!"

[pause] "That life is behind me. [pause] I was a king for 86 days 10 years and 22 centuries ago. I'm a TimeWatch agent now."

"How can you work for the people who let Tudor kill us, marry our sister, and steal your crown?"

"TimeWatch didn't let anyone kill us. You're here, aren't you? Instead of in the Garden Tower smothered under a pillow? TimeWatch got us out."

"*Kate* got us out. The rest of TimeWatch would have left us there. I don't know what the hell is wrong with you that you think we owe them anything, but I don't need a place in the world badly enough to lick their boots."

"Get in the autochron. We're going home."

"It's not my home."

[end tether recording]

3612 CE: THOMAS WU
TimeWatch headquarters

Symond's gone. I blame myself; I should have personally escorted her to the infirmary last night. I should have recognized her raving about internal conspiracy as a sign of temporal fatigue, instead of attributing it to too much wine on top of too little sleep.

Now she's out there somewhere in time and space, fled or subsumed, suffering from the psychological effects of borderline chronal instability. (She *must* be. Because the alternative is that she's right, and we've been infiltrated by – No, that simply can't be the case. Temporal fatigue.)

Obviously we need to bring her back for treatment, but no one has any idea where or when she has gone, and "all of history" isn't a reasonable searching ground. If I thought a particular time or place or person would draw her, I'd look there first, but there isn't –

Oh. That's an idea. Maybe there could be.

I think I'll go pay myself a visit.

«later»

Dodging the paradoxes was a little challenging, but all's well. Looking through my personal journal, I see that I did indeed acquiesce to Richard Plantagenet's desire to leave TimeWatch, and that he has spent the past three years living in 1950s New York.

Now I have a place to watch. Symond will go to him if she'll go to anyone, and we'll scoop her up and bring her home.

Come to think of it, I expect a lot of rogue time travelers would go to Richard

for help.
> Now I have a place to look for them, too.
> I should have thought of this sooner.

end

RICHARD PLANTAGENET.

PRINTER'S NOTE

On 1st May 1895 a young gentlemen – a recently admitted solicitor from the West Country – called upon the offices of Pelgrane Press bearing a manuscript loosely bound in waxed paper and string, together with a small steamer trunk packed with an assortment of curios. Acting under instructions from his anonymous client, he passed these items to me together with a banker's draft drawn on the Bank of England for a substantial sum. The latter overcame my misgivings at such unusual arrangements, so we set the manuscript illustrated with the associated items, and sent it to press. In just under a month, the entire run of books is to be collected by the same young man.

I am no critic – my customers would not tolerate such a thing – but the book itself is a work of scientific romance, a gallimaufry of fables in the manner of Jules Verne, or that more recent publication, 'The Time Machine' by H. G. Wells, but it lacks their grand design and reminds me more of a commonplace book. To what end it was written, and for whom, I may never know, but I hope you, Gentle Reader, find it of use, whoever you are, wherever you may travel and whenever you read it.

O. P.

12th February, 1892

INTERIOR ART

Juha Makkonen

    p.5. Tourists Observe the Dinosaur Extinction Event.

    p. 19. Hannibal Turns the Tide at Zama.

    p. 41. An Agent is Recruited, San Francisco Earthquake 1906.

    p. 51. The Third Robot Uprising, Paris.

    p. 53. A Duel During the Paradox of 2142.

Sarah Wroot

    p. 75. Edward V. Clockwise from top: Long Island Rail Road ticket, 1960s redrawn from eBay LongIslandRR.s-l1600.jpg; fragment of Toyson alchemical frontispiece; Victorian cut steel button; ammonite fossil charm; cross.

    p. 81. Ambrose Bierce. Clockwise from top: 20th century yale key on tablet-woven silk ribbon; mexican onyx turtle; sun purple glass; unknown capsules.

    p. 95. Agent Snow. One dead white rose.

    p.115. Theodosia Burr. Top: personal photo; below left, gold brooch set with pearl 1850-1910; below right, bone frog.

    p. 137. Templeton Graves. Shotglass from Goldfield, Nevada.

    p. 165. Engineer Pritesh. Top: XXIII Olympiad ticket; below, Venetian glass gold foil heart.

    p. 185. Liu Feyan. Top: carved bone moon from indonesia; below, paua or abalone shell from New Zealand or western North America.

    p. 217. Katia Filipovna. Top: Fossil coral; below, badge of the 15th-century Order of the Dragon founded in 1408 by Sigismund of Hungary to combat the infidel.

    p. 229. Richard Plantagenet. Top: fragment of parchment containing excerpt of 14th-century antiphonary music manuscript; below left, desert pavement from Death Valley; below right, silver limpet charm from 20th-century Orkney.

All other artwork is in the public domain.